THOM S. RAINER
& ART RAINER

RAISING DAD

WHAT FATHERS & SONS
LEARN FROM EACH OTHER

PUBLISHING GROUP
Nashville, Tennessee

ISBN: 978-0-8054-4391-2

Published by B&H Publishing Group,
Nashville, Tennessee

Dewey Decimal Number: 306.874
Subject Heading: MEN \ FATHERS AND SONS \ BOYS

1 2 3 4 5 6 7 8 9 10   10 09 08 07

— From Art —

To my wife:
Sarah, I love you. You inspire me to move, to be the man you know I can be. In every way, you are beautiful.

To my mother:
Mom, you make God smile. Thank you for your dedication to your family. Great things are planned for you; it is only the beginning. I love you.

— From Thom —

To Art, Sam, and Jess:
You are the three greatest sons in the world. You raised your dad well.

To Nellie Jo:
You make me smile too. The years of marriage only get better. Thank you for raising these boys and letting me get some undeserved credit in this book.

To Sarah, Erin, and Rachel:
Welcome to the Rainer family. You are such blessings to our sons and to Nellie Jo and me.

To Peggy "Sue" Dutton:
You loved Art, Sam, and Jess as if they were your own grandchildren.

Books by Thom S. Rainer

Raising Dad (coauthor)
Simple Church (coauthor)
The Unexpected Journey
Breakout Churches
The Unchurched Next Door
Surprising Insights from the Unchurched
Eating the Elephant, rev. ed. (coauthor)
High Expectations
The Every Church Guide to Growth (coauthor)
The Bridger Generation
Effective Evangelistic Churches
The Church Growth Encyclopedia (coeditor)
Experiencing Personal Revival (coauthor)
Giant Awakenings
Biblical Standards for Evangelists (coauthor)
Eating the Elephant
The Book of Church Growth
Evangelism in the Twenty-first Century (editor)

TABLE OF CONTENTS

Foreword

I met Thom Rainer in the spring of 1994. As a graduate student at The Southern Baptist Theological Seminary, I was assigned to pick him up at the airport. Thom was an emerging scholar in the field of church growth and had just been tabbed as the founding dean of the Billy Graham School of Missions, Evangelism, and Church Growth at The Southern Baptist Theological Seminary. We weren't in the car five minutes before Thom began to tell me stories about his wife and his boys. I was immediately impressed by the love with which he spoke about his family. By the end of the brief journey between the Louisville airport and Southern Seminary, I knew that Thom Rainer was a family man worthy of my admiration and respect. Little did I know that one encounter would be the beginning of a lifelong friendship.

I first came to know Thom as his student—sitting in his classes, occasionally being asked to help with special projects, often recruited as a willing "gofer," required to buy and read his books for class every semester. I had multiple opportunities to watch him in action as a professor, dean, and influential denominational leader. Of course, I learned a lot from all of those experiences. But the times that made the biggest impression on me were the times I got to see Thom love his family. I have sat with him at his sons' basketball and football games where his passion for his boys' athletic endeavors occasionally erupted in what I would call "Christian fussing" (all Christian dads can understand what this phrase means), and I have shared many laughs with Thom and his family. I have always watched carefully as he treated Nellie Jo with tenderness and respect. Although I have learned much from Dr. Rainer in the arenas of the academy and the formal ministry, his finest lessons have always been the seamless integration of Thom's love for Christ, his love for the church, and his love for his wife and children.

With all of that being said, I am not surprised at all that Art and Thom would write this amazing book together. Art's love and respect for his Dad come through loud and clear, and Thom's characteristic humility and sense of humor are evident throughout. The thing that makes this book great is their willingness to be transparent, not only to one another, but to their readers as well. This book is a great tribute to the relationship that one father shares with his son, but it is also a display of the honor and reverence with which all of the Rainer men hold Nellie Jo. On nearly every page, Art and Thom point to her behind-the-scenes leadership in daily family life. Those of us who are privileged to know her can testify that she is worthy of every word.

Over the last twelve years I have had a front row seat as Thom's speaking, writing, and consulting career have grown in an amazing way. In that time he founded and nurtured a school, published numerous books, and has become president of a half-billion dollar Christian resources company. But through all of those successes, Thom's top priorities have remained his roles as husband and father. In 1994, Thom was still in his thirties, the father of three young boys and the husband of a beautiful wife. I was a twenty-one-year-old single guy, just hoping to survive seminary. Now, Thom is a rapidly aging empty nester (although Nellie Jo remains young and beautiful), and I am the happily married father of six children—five boys and a girl (six is all we have now, but who knows what the future holds?). I knew him first as my dean; as I grew up we became colleagues; and now we remain close friends. My admiration and appreciation for what he and Nellie Jo have accomplished with their sons has only grown. It's funny, while Art, Sam, and Jess were busy raising their dad, in many ways they were helping to raise other dads as well, spectators to the Rainer family who hope and pray that we can emulate in our families the kind of warmth, commitment, and godliness that their family embodies.

As I read Raising Dad, my thoughts kept returning to Psalm 127. In that beautiful hymn, David wrote that children are a blessing. It is obvious to all that know the Rainers that Art, Sam, and Jess are a blessing to many, and especially to their parents. At the end of the psalm it talks about a man's highest achievement, that his grown sons are proud to stand "at the gate" with their father. In this book, Art, along with his brothers, are publicly "going to the gate" with their dad. Well done, Thom and Nellie Jo; you raised three fine boys who are now three fine men. Well done, boys; you have raised a great dad. You are a great encouragement to your readers. Hopefully we can go and do likewise.

Jimmy Scroggins
Dean, Boyce College
Teaching Pastor, Highview Baptist Church

ACKNOWLEDGMENTS

What a scary and fun time it is to put pieces of your life on paper for everyone to read! When I approached my dad with this idea, I had no clue what would soon transpire. It has been an incredible journey from the introduction to the final chapter, sorting through memories of a childhood that refused to be forgotten. During the writing process, I laughed and cried about moments in time that have come and gone. Even if it is not for a book, I recommend that everyone take some time to reflect on what has already taken place in your life. Memories can be quite powerful, and you might be surprised at what comes out.

To state the obvious, without my dad there would be no book. He provided a lifetime of fond memories from which I could pull. He believed in me and wholeheartedly stood behind the development of this book. His desire to see the writing to completion fueled the fire that had already been placed in me. These pages cannot contain the gratitude I have for my father. I feel so blessed yet so undeserving at the same time.

He made this experience a complete joy. I will never forget the moments we have shared throughout this process.

There is another story hidden within the pages of this book. It is a story of a wife and mother who dedicated her life to her family. It is a story of a woman who was able to raise not only her children, but her husband as well. My mom is an amazing lady; anyone who meets her knows this. I love her and am grateful for her impact on my life. My pride in my mother and the life she continues to live cannot be expressed in words. I am grateful that I have the opportunity to see this woman live out such a holy life.

At the time of this writing, my wife and I celebrate our first month of marriage together. Sarah is my inspiration. I cannot imagine a better mate for my life; she is absolutely amazing. Sarah is proof that God knows exactly what He is doing when He puts two people, running after Him, together. During this entire process, she has continuously encouraged me. She was more understanding than any wife should be, for I am sure that the time I spent writing has taken a toll on her as well. I love her and need her for the rest of my life.

I must express a tremendous amount of appreciation to the LifeWay family, specifically B&H Publishing Group. From the first time I stepped through their doors, their warmth surrounded me. They are incredible people, and I am blessed to have worked with them on this project.

My greatest desire goes toward Jesus, my Savior. This life He has given me is one great adventure. I cannot imagine living for anyone or anything else.

Art Rainer

How does one express in words a joy that comes from receiving one of the greatest honors of his life? Such is the situation in which I find myself. I never would have asked one of my sons to write this book with me. I knew that I did not deserve it.

So when Art said he wanted to write a book on fatherhood with me, I was overwhelmed with joy. I love that son of mine so much. Through this project, he has given me something that I will treasure all of my years. Thank you, Art. You have done something indescribably great for your old man.

Art did raise his dad well. But he was not alone. Sam and Jess also did their parts, and I love and appreciate them. Three great sons. What a blessing! What an incredible blessing.

The words that Art wrote about his mother were right on target. When you read this book, you will see that Art has a positive opinion of me and my attempts at fatherhood. But we both know the truth. My wife, Nellie Jo, is the true heroine. She sacrificed so much to raise our three boys. Her love towards them and me is something to behold. All four of your "boys" love you, Nellie Jo. You are truly one great lady.

I so much appreciate the B&H team and the great work they are doing in my publishing ventures. It is a joy to be at LifeWay Christian Resources. I never take a day for granted.

Before I conclude these acknowledgments, I must say a word about three terrific young ladies: Sarah, Erin, and Rachel. God has blessed Nellie Jo and me with three of the most beautiful and wonderful daughters-in-law. I love these three girls. I love how my boys love their wives. And I love how the wives love them. Finally—Nellie Jo has some other females in the family.

A special thanks to the readers of this book. If you have read any of my previous books, you will note that this one is a bit out of my genre. But if you have read my books or heard me speak, you also know that I can't go long without talking about my family. Now you get to see us up close—for better and worse. I pray that our journey will help you on yours. Thanks for being here with us.

Thom S. Rainer

~~~~~~~~~

Creating Raising Dad

Sometimes I like to be alone. In fact, I have abandoned my everyday life for solitude a couple of times. It's not that I don't enjoy the company of others or that I don't like people. Actually, I love people. There are just times when I feel I need to get away from everything, to be by myself for a while. Sometimes I feel I can't hear myself think with all the noise and distractions that are surrounding me. You can probably relate. I get bogged down with work, school, and relationships; all good things, but too much of the combination can leave me weary.

When my freedom seems to disappear and I start to feel like I have lost who I am, that's when I need to somehow connect once again. I do not leave like a madman, slamming the door and squealing the tires as I jet unexpectedly. These are planned trips, and I inform my wife and family in advance of my upcoming journey. Fortunately, they know me and understand my intentions.

The few times I have done this I have chosen Florida as my hideaway. I take the trip from Lexington, Kentucky, down to Florida by myself. The drive is great. I get about twelve straight hours to think, listen to music, and talk to God before I reach my destination. Thanks to wireless phone headsets, I no longer look crazy to other drivers when I converse with God. I fit right in. The other drivers probably think I am on the phone with someone. I guess, in a way, I am.

While in Florida, I usually spend a couple of days just reading, praying, and rummaging through my thoughts. I take walks on the beach and think about God and my life—where I have been and where I am going. As I watch the waves roll in from the Gulf of Mexico, I sometimes wonder how God is going to use me next, and sometimes I simply marvel at the sheer power, creativity, and graciousness of the Lord I serve.

It is also during these trips that different ideas or thoughts enter my mind. They seem to come from nowhere, randomly placed in my head. Sometimes they are inspired by a song I recently heard or a Bible verse I read. Sometimes they just come. One moment I am looking at the ocean or a flawless sunset, and suddenly I am bombarded with ideas about a new business that I could create or a book I could write. I try to jot these ideas down in case I want to pursue them someday. Few ever see the light of day, but some do. Either way, it's fun to dream about the possibilities.

One afternoon I was lying on a chair outside while reading a book whose title and purpose I cannot recall right now. I do know that it wasn't about parenting, because up to that point, having children was the farthest thing from my mind, and I had no desire to read on the topic. But somehow I did start to think about my family. The more I thumbed through the pages of my mind, the more I realized that my family is somewhat of an anomaly in today's society. My parents, two brothers, and I are different, but in a good way. I have been blessed with two parents who are able to celebrate thirty years of life together. This has been their one and only marriage—something that only happens in about 50 percent of marriages in the United States.

My brothers and I have turned out fine. We didn't have any major troubles while growing up and are now successful, each in his own way. Our family remained close throughout my childhood, and even now, living in different cities, we stay connected. In fact, when I looked at the way my parents raised me, I realized that I wouldn't change a thing. That seemed weird. What was the secret that made that possible? Sure, there are probably plenty of families who can claim success, and just because a family goes through hard times or has trouble does not mean that they have failed.

Still, I was amazed at my family.

I guess I had never really thought about it before. Maybe it was because I am now older and more able to appreciate the life I have lived. I always thought my family was normal, nothing special, but maybe we are not so normal after all.

As I sat there with my feet digging into the soft, white sand, I wondered: *Is there something to our family? Should our story be told? Could, in some way, the story of childrearing that I have seen make a difference in someone else's life? Could my experiences of how I was raised matter? Could it be put on paper?*

The more I thought about it, the more I felt that I needed to do this. I needed to check this thing out. I jotted down a few notes to see where these ideas would take me. My relationship with my parents is close, and both of them have done an incredible job in my development. I could have written about my mother just as easily. She is an amazing woman of God. I have told her that she is one of the few people I can clearly imagine making God smile when He watches her live out her life. I could not have asked for a better mother.

However, at this point it seemed best to focus on what my father did right while raising me to be the man that I now attempt to be. With my father's writing experience, I felt that this idea had a better shot at becoming reality.

The development of the book was easy. There were so many areas in my childhood that I felt he did correctly that I had no difficulty creating topics that we could explore. My pen wrote feverishly as it tried to keep up with the ideas that were running through my head.

I called my dad to see what he thought about the idea.

"Dad, I have an idea for a book."

"Great! What is it?"

"It's about us."

"You and me?"

"Right. It is about what you did right during my childhood, and I will need your help. I think people need to know our story."

We continued to talk as I went into the idea in greater detail.

Obviously, my father loved the idea. He, too, believed that this book could be written not to brag, flaunt, or say that his ways were perfect, but to provoke thought in the minds of its readers on the topic of child rearing—to take the good and the bad that my father did and apply it to their own families.

Though neither of us is a child psychologist, my father and I both have the experience to provide some insight into how a real father-son, parent-child relationship can work. We would provide real-life happenings in the history of a bond between a dad and his son that is still growing deeper with every passing year. This would not be regarded as a "how to" book, but more as a reading on "how they did." Obviously, not everything that was done in my childhood would work without a hitch in another's life. We would expect different readers to get totally different insights about their own families. And that would be the beauty of the book; it could be applied in some way and somehow to every parent or parent-to-be. My father and I approached this book with excitement, greatly anticipating the end result.

A thought ran through my mind while I was at church one Sunday morning. It had nothing to do with the sermon, though I am sure that the message the pastor shared was rich and applicable, but it did have everything to do with parenting. It was a somewhat humbling thought for someone who was going to write a book about a father-son relationship. Realizing that God has already provided us with the ultimate parenting handbook, whatever is contained in the pages of our book could not compare to that which has already been written.

The Bible is a real story of a Father and His dedication, love, and sacrifice for His children. When taken as a whole, it becomes the ultimate guide for parents. It is a love story like no other. If parents were to take the Bible and engrave its teachings in their hearts and minds so that its powerful words influence every decision they made and every thought that entered their mind, there would be no need for any supplementary reading.

Perhaps this is why I had such a desire to bring this book to fruition. For me, the relationship shared between my dad and me has given me a taste of the love that our God has for us. Though the depth of the love pales in comparison to God's love for His children, I believe it is a sample. Maybe I was also starting to realize that engraving God's Word on his heart and mind is exactly what Dad did, and this would be a way to celebrate what God can do for those parents who unceasingly chase after Him. Maybe this would be more of a celebration than anything—a celebration of the incredible relationship that can exist between parent and child when God is allowed to get involved, when we allow Him to crash our self-righteous, self-sufficient party.

For the record, I normally pay attention in church. I go to an amazing church that teaches about God and the Bible. The pastor, Jon, is deep in intellect and heart, and I hate missing him speak. Having said that, let's continue.

THE SET UP

You will soon discover that I have placed my dad on a high pedestal and have an extremely biased view on the way he raised me. I say this unashamedly and I exude appreciation for my father and what he has done in my life. I anticipated this view-point coming through in my writing, which is one of the many reasons why I wanted to include my father in this writing. He helps bring a little reality into the book.

Each chapter is divided into two parts. The first half of the chapter is my view as a child on issues that my father dealt with well. So many books are written from an adult's perspective, and there are many good things that come from these writings.

However, I wanted this book to be different. I wanted parents to be able to read what I saw and thought as a child. There was no better time for me to write these experiences than now. I am still young enough to remember well the images and feelings of my childhood, yet I am old enough to articulate what was then occurring in my life.

With each part I write, you will discover the times where I applaud Dad for my upbringing. Every chapter is dedicated to a subject matter, an area in a child's life, that I determined my father handled correctly. I tried to make sure that the topics we address are applicable for all parents so that the information given is meaningful.

My dad and I determined that the first half of each chapter had to be completed before the second half was written, this leaving room for spontaneity in the latter part. You will soon see that each chapter was set up with a point and a counterpoint.

The second half of each chapter is my father's response to my view of the upbringing I received from my dad. While the first part consists of the praise of my father, the second part plugs some reality into the book. My father shares with us the "behind the scenes" look at what really went on in the parenting world of Thom Rainer. He shares both the successes and the mistakes of his life as a father, and with each chapter, he brings some lessons that he has learned while bringing up three children.

Our hope is that you are able to find ways in which you can relate to our stories and uncover teachings from Thom Rainer's school of real-life child raising. You may choose to implement some lessons in your life as a parent and choose to ignore others. It is up to you. All that we can do is tell you our story in hopes of your unlocking some truth that was hidden before you chose to turn these pages.

To the Reader

Thank you for picking up this book. Without an audience, it would have no purpose. We appreciate the time you have given us to reveal a little bit about our lives to you. You have provided us a great opportunity, and though we may not know your story, we pray that God will lead you in this reading to find that for which you are searching.

Art Rainer

Chapter 1

~~~~~~~~

Raising Dad:
Memories and More

This is the last chapter in the book, or at least it should be. In fact, by all logic, this section really would be great as the conclusion, and it could easily summarize all that follows this chapter. You might even consider reading this again, after you have finished the book. A perfect ending. So why *did* I decide to put this chapter first?

To tell these stories.

It was the spring of 1963, around 3:00 p.m., and Thom (pronounced "Tom") had just arrived home from school.

In the small, slow, southern Alabama town known as "The Bird Dog Capital of the World," businesses closed down a little earlier than they do today, and Thom knew that his dad, for whom he had the utmost admiration, would be home soon.

You see, Thom's dad fit the image of the greatest of men for that day. He had fought in World War II as a gunner on a B-24 bomber and had earned two Purple Hearts for his heroic efforts while wounded in combat. Now he was a banker and the town's mayor. He was highly revered, a role model for men to equal and children to emulate. He was also unashamed to take unpopular stands for the equality of blacks and whites in an era and state where racial tensions ran high. His character was of the highest standards.

To Thom, his dad was stoic—resisting showing emotions for fear that those emotions would demonstrate weakness. He also showed little overt affection, especially physical affection to his children.

As was Thom's routine when he got home from school, he found the basketball in his family's one-story, ranch-style house, and started shooting at a basketball goal mounted to the side of a tree as he waited for his dad's arrival.

Then, like clockwork, Thom's dad came home, and Thom started to get excited.

He ran to his dad, basketball held tightly, sweat starting to show on his buzzed head from the Alabama heat, and asked with excitement in a voice that only a child could produce, "Dad, do you wanna play some basketball?"

"Not right now, son. I've got to go take a nap."

Thom's dad rarely came back out.

Still 1963, it was now summertime, and that meant two things: baseball and the family vacation to the beach.

Every year Thom's family, which also included older brother Sam along with his mom and dad, loaded the family car and ventured to Florida's Panama City Beach for vacation. Typically, they met up with other families from their small town and rented several motel rooms on the beach.

Every day the families would wake up and head to the beach to allow the children to play in the water and sand while the parents soaked up the Florida sun. Around lunchtime, all of the children were sent to a room to take naps.

On one particular day of this vacation, Thom, one of the youngest in the group, and the other children could not fall asleep for their naps. They became restless as children do and decided to head out to the sand dunes across the street to play. They remembered that their parents had told them not to go into the water alone, but it was generally agreed among the group of kids that they could play on the dunes.

To Thom, the sand dunes seemed to rise like mountains from the beach's sands. They climbed up and down the first couple of dunes and settled on a place to play down in the valleys between the mountains of sand. Time passed and Thom started to become tired. He decided to leave the group of children and head back to the motel. As he climbed to reach the peak of the final dune, he saw that something was going on back at the motel across the street.

Parents were frantically pacing and searching. They looked like a bunch of ants running around whose mound had just been destroyed. Thom quickly realized that they had found the children's nap room empty and could not find the kids because the height of the dunes covered them from the motel's view. Thom knew he was in trouble.

As he stood on top of the dune, he saw his dad look up and point at him. All the parents turned to see Thom as his father started running toward him.

Oddly, the only reaction Thom had was to run to his dad, who was running on a collision course toward him. As they drew closer, Thom saw the familiar look on his dad's face that he saw every time he was headed for trouble. As he ran, tears started flowing from the little boy's eyes because he knew that certain punishment was awaiting him when he met his father. He saw his dad start reaching for his belt. More tears.

As Thom reached for his dad, the hand he had seen reaching for the belt suddenly reached toward him. In an instant, Thom was swooped up into his dad's arms and the running stopped. They stood there, Thom with his little arms not able to reach fully around his father, and his dad, also in tears, arms wrapped tightly around his lost son.

Never had Thom felt so secure and so loved.

Such was the strange relationship between my father, Thom Rainer, and his dad.

I tell you these stories for two reasons. First, to help you understand what type of relationship my father had with his dad. Second, to show the importance of the actions parents take with their children and the memories they create.

Making Memories

Looking back on my relationship with my father, I have countless memories of things we did, places we went, and conversations we had. As I sit here and write, moments of my childhood rush through my head, so many that they are hard to sort through. Amusement parks, beach trips, Little League and high school games, church functions, dinners, and the list goes on and on. All include images of my dad.

If there was one thing my father was good at (and as you read, you will find that I respect him in many different areas), it was making memories. My father seemed to intentionally create times that I could look back on with fondness. Because of this, nearly every conversation and topic brings to mind a moment shared by me and my father.

For instance, whenever a college football game is on, I think about my two brothers, my dad, and me on Saturdays in the fall, sitting around a small, thirteen-inch television, decked out in crimson and white from head to toe, cheering on the University of Alabama Crimson Tide. Even when I was too young to understand what was going on, I loved the excitement of my dad running through the house, screaming, and jumping like a kid whenever the Tide scored a touchdown or got an interception. Until I attended college at the University of Kentucky, I proudly supported the Crimson Tide and happily joined my dad in his crazy game-day shenanigans.

I also remember Little League baseball. My dad was one of the coaches when my older brother, Sam, and I were on the same team. Our team name was the Warriors. Honestly, I don't remember if we were any good. Looking back at pictures with me, cap crooked, shaggy hair flowing, and socks up as far as they would go, I am betting that we were probably not the best team in the league because everyone else on the team, including my brother, looked just as goofy as I did.

However, I do remember practicing and playing the games with my dad. We would hit and throw together. He taught me how to field a ground ball and to throw the ball to the right base. Whenever I did well in a game, he was the first to congratulate me, and when I did not do so well, he was the first to give me a hug.

As I continue to reminisce about my growing up years, I can't help but think what my life would be without my dad. In almost every good memory, he seems somewhat connected, especially when it comes to my earlier childhood. And that is fine because, to me, those are the types of thoughts that should never disappear when the years have passed and the children are grown.

This book is about raising Dad. It is my perspective as a son on what he did well. I will let Dad tell you what he thinks about times he did not do so well. I want to share my story, not because it is more important than yours, but because we probably have some common lessons to learn.

Dad really made memories. Let me just share with you a few of the principles I learned from him as he made so many memories.

He Cared What We, His Sons, Would Think about Him

When I say that my dad cared about what we would think of him, I am not suggesting that my father wanted to be the "cool" dad on the street. In fact, back then I couldn't believe anyone would classify my dad as cool. I saw him as most children see their father, one big geek. (You should see some of the thigh-high shorts and massive glasses he used to wear back in the '80s! Not cool, even by '80s standards.)

There are many fathers who are so concerned about being liked by their children that they allow their kids to grow up practically independent of parental guidance. They think that staying out of their kids' lives will help them maintain good relationships with their children. They declare it "freedom" for their children. I remember growing up with some of my peers who had fathers who stayed at an arm's distance from their children's lives, and I admit, at the time, I wished that my dad would sometimes do the same. However, in hindsight, that is one of the saddest situations that could occur in relationships between father and son or daughter. I am glad that my father chose to be a part of my life.

You see, my dad cared about how my brothers and I would remember him as we grew up to be adults. He was determined not to engrave the memories, as his father had, of being too busy to spend time with his children. The images of his childhood would not be repeated in the lives of his kids. My dad longed to fill our minds with pleasant memories that we could hold on to and one day tell our children. After all, when a human passes away, memories are all that are left on this side of eternity.

He Was Purposeful

As I said before, I think that my dad made memories on purpose. Let me give you this example.

When I was a kid, there was just something magical about a clown and two golden arches. Call it the effect of the commercials during Saturday morning cartoons being engraved into an innocent child's brain or whatever you want to, but I loved those Happy Meals. (For all of the health-conscious readers, do not get me wrong; my parents did not take me to McDonald's very often, so when they did, it was a real treat.)

When I was younger, my father decided he wanted to spend one-on-one time with his three sons. What he chose to do was take each one of us, individually, to breakfast at McDonald's on alternating Saturday mornings. Now this might not seem like a big deal to you, but to us three boys, it was enough to keep us up at night before the morning of our turn. We were able to get the food we loved and spend time with our dad alone. Nothing could be better!

This was intentional. I now have fond memories of spending Saturday mornings with my dad at McDonald's because he made a purposeful attempt at creating some memories.

He Did It for Us

As you will soon learn in this book, my dad was unselfish when it came to his family. The only time the family took the backseat with any issue was when Dad felt God's calling on his life to do something or to go somewhere. The same was true when it came to his resolute decision to make sure that we had good recollections of him.

My dad did not do these things so that he could brag to his friends or church buddies about being the greatest dad, and I never saw him care what others thought about the time he dedicated to his children, for good or bad. The truth is that I saw my dad doing all of this for us, his boys. I do not even think that he cared about his memories as long as he knew his children were going to look back on their time spent under his guidance as a series of moments that they would like to repeat one day with their children.

The Memory Making Never Stops

Even today, Dad seems to continue making memories purposefully. And believe it or not, some of my favorite recollections have occurred since I have grown and left the house. The fact is that even as my relationship with my father has changed from parental figure to best friend, he continues to seek new ways in which to create lasting moments and further our relationship. The best current example?

You're reading it.

— A Father's Perspective —

I (Thom) received three major doses of grace in my lifetime. The first took place right after football practice when I was in high school. Coach Joe Hendrickson introduced me to the Savior I knew little about. Later that evening, I grasped fully the concept of grace.

I did not deserve salvation through Jesus Christ. I am a sinner whose sins put Jesus on the cross. But He loved me anyway. And when I repented of my sins and accepted the free gift of salvation through faith in Christ, I also learned about grace. It is unmerited favor, receiving something you do not deserve.

The second dose of grace came my way on December 17, 1977. My wife said, "I do," and my life has been richer and happier than I could ever deserve. Her love is a gift of grace. It is something I do not deserve, but for which I will be forever grateful.

Three sons named Sam, Art, and Jess gave me the third major dose of grace. Somehow, someway, they love and respect me despite the many times I have blown it. They say great things about me, but I know I have many times failed them and their mother.

You see, I am a father who is so far from perfect that I wonder what I did to receive such love from my sons. And how could I ever deserve a co-authored book with Art that speaks of me with such adulation?

Each time I read Art's part of these chapters, I fight tears. Love is an amazing thing. It obviously keeps no record of wrongs. It is patient. It is kind. And it is giving. That is the grace I see when I read Art's words. That is the love I feel.

You, the reader, will hear my response to each of Art's chapters. You will hear my many struggles. And you will hear a few of my victories.

Art took you back to my childhood in the 1960s. Let me fast forward to the 1970s, when I learned some important lessons about being a father, even before my first child was born.

Lessons from James Dobson

My excitement was palpable. My wife, Nellie Jo, called me to tell me the tests were positive. She was pregnant. I was going to be a father!

Wait a minute! I was going to be a father? I was a twenty-four-year-old clueless kid. How could I possibly handle the responsibility of a child? Where were the directions for this new venture?

The year was 1979. The town was Anniston, Alabama. By February 1980, my life would change dramatically as the first of three sons arrived.

I did have two important lessons from my own parents. The first lesson was one of the greatest gifts a parent can give a child. Both Mom and Dad encouraged me continuously. They built me up and contributed greatly to my self-esteem. I thought I could conquer the world because my parents told me I could.

When I hear parents berating their kids today, I want to scream "No!" at the top of my lungs. I know the gift of encouragement. And I have also seen the destructive effects of negative words by parents on their children.

But the second lesson I learned from my parents was not positive. Art alluded to it earlier. Most of the time they, particularly Dad, were just too busy for me. And his busyness included naps, fishing, and hunting. I had trouble working into his schedule.

I was determined that I would learn both lessons from my parents and apply them to my own children. I would encourage them and build them up. And I would give them the time I so desperately wanted with my own father.

But there is so much more to raising kids. Where was the handbook?

In 1979 that question was answered at least in part. My church, Golden Springs Baptist Church, was providing a film series over several weeks by an up-and-coming Christian psychologist named James Dobson. The name of the film series was *Focus on the Family*.

I clearly remember sitting in the sanctuary of Golden Springs Baptist Church on consecutive Sunday evenings and soaking in every word Dr. Dobson said. It was a crash course on parenting. Though no course could offer everything you need to know, it was a godsend to me. Even to this day, I remember stories and lessons from *Focus on the Family*.

If there was an overarching theme that I remember from Dr. Dobson, it was the importance of the present. As a husband and a father, what I did this day would create memories, for better and worse, in the lives of my wife and children. I would learn from the mistakes of my own father, and I would create moments that my family would cherish for the rest of their lives.

Sounds great, doesn't it? Well, perhaps I succeeded some of the time, but can I call my memory-making fatherhood a complete success?

Hardly.

SOME BAD MEMORIES

The job offer seemed too good to be true. And I think I discerned God's will the best I could. My family would move from the comfort of friends and schools to a new location some four hundred miles away.

I was having the time of my life. The new work surpassed my expectations. I was one happy guy. I would return from my workplace each day with a whistle and a kick in my step.

But my family was suffering: a new town, a new culture, new schools, and friends left behind.

Bad memories.

I returned from work in my usual jovial mood. My life was great. I ran up the steps to the boys' rooms to greet them. Two of the boys were gone. But Art was in his room.

The door was almost closed. I opened it slowly and looked in.

There was my twelve-year-old son on the floor face down. Crying softly.

"What's the matter, buddy?" I asked gently.

The tear-strewn face said it all. But his words made it even more poignant. "Dad, I am so lonely."

You see, to this day I still think the job relocation was the right thing to do, but I also know I did the move the wrong way.

I delved into my work from day one. I gave my all to my new vocation. And my family suffered, mostly in silence.

It is hard for me to look back on those days and see what an incredible jerk I was. I should have given my family more time. I should have introduced them more fully to the new town that was their reluctant home.

Instead, I enjoyed my new work while my family hurt.

"Dad, I am so lonely."

Bad memories.

THE MEMORY-MAKING TENSION

I am a father and husband who has constantly struggled with balance, particularly in the area of work and family. To hear Art's perspective, you might think that I could simply put my vocational work aside and give complete memory-making time to my family.

Throughout my adulthood and fatherhood, I *have* been intentional about creating memories for my boys. Art is correct on that point. But what he left out is how I struggle with taking time to do that with my family versus taking time for my work.

Let me give you an example.

Art spoke about the McDonald's adventures the three boys and I had for a season. OK, I will give myself some credit. I did create those memory-making moments on Saturday mornings. I was intentional about spending time with my boys one-on-one.

But Art doesn't remember the Saturday morning crisis.

It was Sam's turn to go to McDonald's. He woke up with anticipation and excitement on that warm winter day in

St. Petersburg, Florida. Shortly before we were to leave, the telephone rang. The cursed phone.

I was the pastor of a growing church in the area. One of our new members had a struggling marriage and I had met with him at least five times to this point. That Saturday morning call was from the new member. His marriage was at a crisis point. Again. Would I meet with him right then?

Please understand. I do not take lightly the problems of his marriage. I know that this man was hurting deeply. But, frankly, he did not need me to be his messiah of the moment.

Do you want to guess what I did? I told the church member that I would meet him in my office in thirty minutes. I quickly told Sam that I had an "emergency" at church, but that I would give him his turn the next week. I left in a rush despite the disappointment I saw in his eyes.

I did take my son to McDonald's the next week. But I still will never forget the hurt on his face.

Bad memories.

MEMORY-MAKING LESSONS FROM A BATTLE-SCARRED DAD

I don't deserve this book, but I accept it as a gift of grace. I don't deserve Art's adulation, but I cherish it nevertheless.

I have learned many lessons, though. My sons have done a good job of raising their dad. Let me share with you some thoughts on this subject.

1. Life is incredibly brief. Being the father of children at home is even briefer. Make the most of those moments because the empty nest is just around the corner.

2. Don't forsake opportunities to make memories with your family because you think you are indispensable elsewhere, particularly at work. I met with the new church member more than a dozen times. His marriage still failed.

3. Your employers quickly forget the long hours you give them at work. Your children never forget the memory-making moments you have with them.

4. Always check your motives. Many times I neglected my family and justified my hours elsewhere because I was the "provider of the family." But the reality is that often I was enjoying the ego trip of being needed.

5. Never communicate with your actions that other people are more important than your family.

MEMORIES: THE GIFT GOES ON

The date was July 16, 2005. My fiftieth birthday had come far too quickly. All the boys were home for the day, a rare treat for me since they are on their own with their own homes.

After gifts were given to me, after some of the most hilarious cards were read, and after the cookie cake was cut, the boys told me that they had one more gift for me.

They asked me to sit down, as they placed a video in the computer. They hit "play." For the next five minutes I watched and listened to a tribute to me. Each of the boys had contributed photos from their birth to the present, and each of them had words of tribute to me.

When it was done, I held my head in my hands and wept.

The music to the video tribute was a song by Keith Urban called "Song for Dad." Some of the lyrics I heard were:

The older I get
The more I can see
How much he loved my mother and my brother
   and me
And he did the best that he could
And I only hope when I have my own family
That every day I see
A little more of my father in me.

On that day I discovered something amazing. My sons were doing what I had attempted to do while they were growing up. They were making memories.

Yeah, I messed up quite a bit, but I guess I did something right.

Grace is truly an amazing thing.

Chapter 2

~~~~~~

When a Father
Is Like the Father

Let's start a chapter on spiritual issues by addressing the most important issue of all: the decision to follow Christ.

My father was one of the tremendous influences, if not *the* influence, in my accepting Jesus Christ to be the Lord of my life. By growing up in the church and having a father who was a minister, it may seem that I had an unfair advantage. Nonetheless, telling someone about the love of Christ is not always easy, and sometimes it is even more difficult to share with a family member. You may or may not have to see a stranger again, but with a family member, you know come Thanksgiving that you are going to be asking them to pass the sweet potatoes your way. Even more, you must continue living with the person under the same roof. However, it is beyond argument that this must be done. Parents must share with their children the grace that Christ's death has given us all.

I did not decide to become a Christian because my dad was a pastor. What led me to make my decision could happen to any child. I became a Christian at the early age of seven because I grew up in a home that sought God, His morals, and His principles. My parents would not allow anything to stand in the way of their children developing a relationship with their God.

———

Our family had just moved to the St. Petersburg, Florida, area the summer before I started first grade. My dad had taken the senior pastor position at a local church, and after coming from the midsection of the United States this seemed like paradise to my young mind. There was warmth in the air, palm trees, and an ocean that appeared to reach the edge of the earth. Everything was new and exciting to my family.

The church was loving and welcoming, and the pastorate provided a great opportunity for my father to spread his wings and put into practice all that he had been taught in seminary. For housing, the church graciously provided a small, one-story, three-bedroom house since the pay did not allow us to afford one of our own. Life in Florida was good.

The school year was soon upon us, and I started my first year in grade school. Even though I was young, I clearly remember my time spent at the local public school, which was only minutes from our house. Yes, my mind is filled with memories of those *two* days I spent there.

You see, my parents made a choice that would affect them, especially financially, for the rest of my schooling.

My first elementary school experience still seems odd to me. We switched classes for every subject, just like students do in most high schools. Granted, we stayed with the same group of children throughout the entire day, but we constantly had different teachers and classrooms. Therefore, we did not end the day in the same room where we started the day. So as my first day of school came to an end, my mother—who was unaware of the switching of classrooms—came to pick up her son as she had done many times before with my older brother.

She arrived a few minutes early and glanced in the room where she had left me earlier that morning. I was not there. She searched a few more classrooms filled with children—not there either. As any mother would, she started to panic. Frantically, she opened the door to an art room where the teacher had yet to dismiss the students. Interrupting the teacher, my mother asked if her son, Art Rainer, was in the class.

The teacher glared back at my mother and said some words to her that I will not repeat in this book, briefly noting that I was in the classroom. My mom, shocked, shut the door and waited outside for the class to conclude.

I sat there silenced, not knowing what to do or say.

Funny, I can still remember a little girl turning to me and asking, "Was that your mom?" Confused at what had just transpired, I nodded. A lump in my throat had formed. I wanted to cry.

I only went to that school one more day. My parents promptly enrolled my brother and me in a private, Christian school—at a tremendous financial burden to them. They decided they would not allow anything but godly models to surround our lives and influence our developing minds. Even though finances were sparse on the minimal income provided by the church, and even as we struggled to pay for groceries, we were sent to a place where God was exalted.

Please do not take this story wrong. If you feel that I am degrading public education and those parents who send their children to public schools, you have missed the point. I have many friends who attended public schools, and they are doing fine. The reason I tell this story is to give an example of my parents wanting God to be in their children's lives so badly that they were willing to take on great sacrifices to make it happen. My parents, specifically my dad, were determined to lead us spiritually.

SPIRITUAL LEADER

Without doubt, my dad was the spiritual leader in our house. This leadership did not come from his biblical or theological knowledge gained in seminary classes or from his pastoral duties. No, this area of guidance came from a genuine desire to be a parent who glorified God in his child rearing. From that inner desire, everything else seemed to follow.

Leading in Prayer

How incredible it must be to kneel by the bedside of your child and share a conversation with God through prayer!

This was commonplace for my father and me. Up until I started middle school, I can hardly remember a night when my dad did not come to my bedside to hear me say my prayers and for me to hear him pray before I went to bed at night.

I recall waiting in my bed on nights when my father would come home late from a church meeting, and even though I knew he was tired and wanting to go to bed, I would yell for him to come into my room because I could not go to sleep until I had my nightly talk with God and my father. It had become a routine that I enjoyed greatly, one that provided many intimate moments that will remain with me for the rest of my life. With the room dark, we prayed to our heavenly Father. This was such a simple act of spiritual leadership, but it made a tremendous impact on my prayer life that is still evident today.

By praying with my dad on a nightly basis, I not only learned the importance of prayer, but I learned *how* to pray. I am still amazed when I come across a Christian friend or acquaintance who admits that he or she does not know how to pray. There seems to be a fear or lack of understanding about the simple act of praying.

Could it be that their only experience with prayer has been hearing a pastor or other ministers pray? Do they associate prayer with listening to only those in church leadership positions?

I am thankful for my father's desire to share his conversations with God because he showed me what prayer is. He laid a solid foundation from which I could build this discipline—and my Christian walk as well.

Leading by Example

To be the spiritual leader in your household, you must lead by example. My father never expected anything from his children that he did not expect from himself. I never heard him use the phrase, "Do as I say and not as I do." And this especially applied to his faith.

My father was an excellent example of someone who backed up his talk with his walk. He not only told us what God and the Bible said about how we, as Christians, should live, but he followed up the words with his life. What he said in the pulpit applied to himself as well as to the congregation.

How confusing it must be for a child to be told by his dad to go to church and learn about Christ while the father stays home to see Sunday's football kickoff. Fathers have a tremendous influence on their child's life. There is such an incredible power, sometimes unknowingly, held by a child's dad. Personally, there were teachers and pastors who made somewhat of an impact on my life, but no one compared to my father. More than his coworkers, more than his congregation, I took his actions to heart more than anyone else. Children look up to their parents to a far greater degree than I believe some adults realize. Parents are the true role models for the next generation.

Fortunately, this is the exact position in which my father wanted to be. He wanted to be the one I looked to for leadership and guidance with my life's choices. When I was confronted with a spiritual matter, he wanted me to look back and remember what he had done in a similar situation. My dad wanted to be my role model, my hero, and he made sure his life was an example to his children—an example where Christ was glorified.

Leading in Evangelism

To say that my father was evangelistic would be an understatement. As pastor and father, it was evident that he was constantly prepared to share the message of Christ, in and out of season. And the fact that he had (and still has) a passion to reach the world goes beyond any ministerial positions he has held. It was and is a true outflow of his heart.

Now how did this evangelistic outpouring affect me as I was growing up? Early on, I learned about sharing and discussing my faith just from watching and listening to my father. The most vivid memory of my father sharing his faith came while we were still living in Florida. It was a Saturday morning and I was, as usual, watching my cartoons.

Then came a knock on our door. Two Jehovah's Witnesses. Did Dad politely say "no thanks" and shut the door? Did he try to make it seem as if no one was at home? Hardly. He saw it as a God-given opportunity.

I listened to my father and the two visitors go back and forth as they discussed each other's beliefs. This lasted for several hours and was, in fact, very entertaining. Yet my mind was like a sponge, absorbing all that was happening before me. And because of numerous instances such as this that I witnessed throughout my childhood, the manner in which I now present the gospel is thankfully similar.

Leading in Tithing

Why finish a chapter concerning spiritual issues with the act of tithing? Out of all the areas from which I could choose, why this one?

To me tithing, or giving, is one of the most important acts in which Christians can outwardly participate. Simply, this is an act of obedience, and the giving of one's possessions is an excellent reflection of one's heart and priorities. Sadly, this basic act is often missed in the teachings of parents.

When I was a child, getting ready each Sunday morning for church would go like this:

1. Wake up.	4. Wake up again.
2. Eat breakfast.	5. Get dressed.
3. Go back to sleep.	6. Get a quarter from my dad.

I would then take the quarter, put it in a church envelope, and travel to church with the family.

From the earliest stages of my life, my father taught me how to give back to God. Even though the few cents I gave were not from my own earnings, I was learning and developing habits for the future. Granted, I did not fully understand the truths about tithing being an act of worship, or that I was glorifying God through my giving. Nonetheless, I was gaining the basic concept that we should give to God as He commanded.

No matter what you want to excel in—athletics, music, writing, or anything else—the longer you do it, the easier it seems and the better you become. The same holds true for giving. My father allowed me to practice tithing early on in my life, and because of this, I feel that I am more readily able to give of myself and my finances. I consider my childhood as the "spring training" of giving, and now that the season has started, it is time to put the lessons learned into action.

As I conclude my portion of this chapter, there is one thing I want to emphasize: Fathers, your children are watching you. From the major to the minor daily decisions you make, your children are constantly engraving your actions into their minds. Be careful. Be purposeful. Be Christ-like. Their eyes are on you, and what you do today will affect their lives in the future.

Be careful, dads. Someone is watching you.

— A Father's Perspective —

The conversation with Art took place shortly before this book was written. It was neither a planned nor a dramatic moment. Just one of those times when he did most of the speaking and I did most of the listening.

I love those moments.

Art's older brother, Sam, had just shared with my wife and me that God was calling him to vocational ministry. Despite his training in finance and business, and despite his success in the business world, he would go to seminary and prepare to be a pastor.

I could not have been prouder.

Art's younger brother, Jess, also a finance major, had made a similar declaration, although he didn't have the certainty of the specifics of the call. He planned to attend seminary as soon as he graduated from college.

I could not have been prouder.

But poor Art. The pressure was on.

His older and younger brothers were both headed for vocational ministry and seminary. They were following the same path taken by their old man.

Would Art be the odd man out in the family?

That is why I so cherished that conversation with Art. He let me know in no uncertain terms that if he sensed God calling him to vocational ministry, he would follow. And though he never articulated it, there was probably some subtle pressure, internal or external, to follow in what Jess calls "the family business."

But Art did not have that calling.

Instead, he had a greater sense of God's direction to make a difference for Him in the business world. Marketplace ministry would be his call.

Though Art has a confidence that needs little assurance, his eyes glanced toward mine as he told me of his own sense of call.

In the two earlier conversations with his brothers, I had an indescribable joy and pride as I heard them share with excitement the paths that God had led them to follow. This time Art described a similar obedience, but a different path.

My reaction? I could not have been prouder.

You see, I have never wanted my sons to do anything other than follow God's will for their lives. I went to seminary with too many young men who seemed to be following family expectations rather than God. Few of them are in ministry today.

I had the same joy hearing Art describe God's direction in his life as I did when his brothers shared a similar conversation.

I could not have been prouder.

A Spiritual Role Model?

Wow! Three great sons who love the Lord. All three of them making a difference for God in their own unique ways. You must have been some kind of spiritual role model, Thom. Tell me how you did it!

If those silly thoughts are going through your mind, let me bring clarity to the situation right away. I was far from the role model Art indicates in this chapter. While I am not suggesting for a moment that my son was fabricating any part of his narrative, I am stating clearly that his memory is blessedly selective.

I am a child of Christ who struggled as a father and who still struggles today.

Let me share but a few of my struggles. The brevity is for my own low tolerance for pain.

Three Sons and God's Word

Almost without exception when the boys were young, we would read together from an illustrated Bible. My sons loved it and so did I. I would read the text and they would look at the pictures as I read. We read through that Bible so many times that the boys memorized many of the stories. And there was at least one illustrated story for each book of the Bible.

I wish I could say that I was dedicated in keeping my boys in the Word. While the illustrated Bible is one positive example, I know of too many omissions. When Art and his brothers were too old to look at a picture Bible, I stopped being consistent in studying the Bible with them. How many times as adolescents did they need their dad sharing truths of Scripture when they were going through the common struggles of their preteen and teenage years?

My leadership in family devotions was worse than inconsistent. It was erratic at best and pathetic at worst.

I have heard of much more devoted fathers sitting with their children at a kitchen table and discussing great truths of Scripture. Oh, I had those discussions with Art and his brothers, but never with the consistency of other fathers.

Today when my adult sons ask me questions about the Scripture, I realize that I should have imparted these truths when they were younger. Like many well-intending parents, I let the church and the Christian schools teach my boys the Word of God oftentimes more than I did myself. And while I am exceedingly grateful for these positive influences in their lives, they should never replace the spiritual leadership of a father.

My parents never discussed the Bible when I was a child. On many occasions I would see my mother reading the Bible, but I have no memory of my father doing so.

When God gave me the gift of three sons, I was determined not to make the same mistakes.

My sons would be led by their father in a deeper understanding of Scripture.

How did I do?

If I were giving myself a grade, I would go with a C.

I read the Bible with them when they were young, and we occasionally had some great discussions about Scripture when they were older.

But I could have done so much better.

Too Busy to Pray

I am writing this chapter on the beautiful and mostly secluded October beaches of Cape San Blas, Florida. My wife and I needed a few days to relax and recharge in the midst of my vocational change to become president of LifeWay Christian Resources and in the midst of our relocation from Louisville to Nashville.

The solitude and the slow pace of the Cape provides me many opportunities to be still and to pray. I woke up early this morning to watch the sun rise and to be alone with God.

It's funny in a not-so-funny way how I have time for God when I have little else on my calendar. I have been able to work Him into my schedule this week with ease.

But this week is a reprieve and an exception. More times than not, I find myself too busy to give my God lengthy times of prayers. Do any of you type A personalities share in my struggles?

As I read Art's words about the joy he had when I prayed with him, I was once again moved to tears. The tears flowed because I also remember how precious those moments were for me with him and his two brothers. I remember teaching them how to pray, and how to appreciate the incredible opportunity to talk to and listen to the One who created us.

"Daddy," he would yell across the house, "I'm ready for you to come hear my prayers." I would sit on his bed or kneel beside it, and a son would hear his father pray to *the* Father. And then I would listen to my own son share his prayers with God.

Precious moments.

Moments never forgotten.

One would think that I would be wise enough to see how prayer powerfully impacted my sons, that I would be a model of a praying man to them. Now, don't get me wrong. I am a man who believes in the power of prayer. I have preached, taught, and exhorted people on the need to have a personal prayer time with God.

It's just that I have not always been the model of consistency in prayer. Sometimes I just get too busy to pray. Writing that previous sentence sends chills of conviction through me. Do you hear what I said? *Sometimes I don't have time for God.* It's ridiculous, isn't it?

I've read the stories of John Hyde, David Brainerd, and David Mueller. I've seen the passion of prayer warriors in the churches I served. Sometimes I seem to get it; other times I don't.

Art concluded his portion of this chapter with two brief and poignant sentences: "Be careful, dads. Someone is watching you."

Did my sons see a praying father who gave first priority to time with God? Or did they see a dad who was inconsistent and sent mixed messages on my own priority of prayer?

I am afraid that if Art were truly to examine the consistent model I offered, he would not be so generous in his assessment of my prayer life.

Too busy to pray? How incredibly dumb was this father who often modeled such a reality.

EVANGELISM IN THE TWENTY-FIRST CENTURY

They offered me a contract! After numerous submissions, a publisher was willing to take a chance on my book. The year was 1988 and the book, to be released in 1989, was *Evangelism in the Twenty-first Century*. Several well-known authors and scholars had agreed to write chapters on topics in evangelism. But the coupe de grace was Billy Graham's willingness to write the foreword to the book.

I had my first book published on a topic for which I was passionate. As I shared in the previous chapter, I developed a passion for sharing my faith when my high school football coach led me to Christ. His passion for Jesus not only was used of God to bring me to Christ, it also gave me an immediate passion for sharing the Good News with others myself.

My boys knew of the high priority I placed on evangelism. When Art's older brother, Sam, was nine years old, I took him with me to a home in St. Petersburg, Florida, the city where I was serving as pastor.

"Sam, I am happy you are going with your daddy, but I need to tell you one thing," I began before we even left our driveway. "The people I have an appointment to visit are not Christians, and your daddy is going to tell them about Jesus. I need you not to interrupt our conversation. OK?" My eldest son smiled and nodded in affirmation.

When we arrived at the home, the couple offered for Sam to play outside in a fenced-in backyard. They showed him the big tree with low-lying limbs that had supported many enthusiastic kids in the past. My son rushed outside with a quick admonition from me for him to be careful.

I had a great conversation with the couple that lasted for nearly an hour. They were eager for me to share the gospel, and they readily prayed to receive Christ. We celebrated together, and then I shared with them the first steps new Christians need to take.

When I was ready to leave, I went out the back door to find Sam. I found my nine-year-old son leaning against a tree with tears flowing down his face. He had fallen from the tree and broken his arm. But he had refused to cry out or to come into the house. Daddy was sharing Jesus and wanted no interruptions.

Of course, I had to apologize to Sam (and my wife) for dogmatically insisting that there be no interruptions. I had to tell my son that I never meant that he could not interrupt me if he really needed me.

But to this day, my sons know the priority I place on evangelism. Right?

Not exactly.

You see, once again I see myself as a model of inconsistency. I talk a good game about evangelism and probably share my faith more than many Christians. But I wonder how many times my sons have seen me *not* share my faith. With strangers at restaurants? With friends at our home? With acquaintances where we do business? With neighbors on our street?

If evangelism was truly the priority I say it is, I would be sharing my faith at every opportunity.

But I have not.

And someone had been watching me.

CONFESSIONS OF A STRUGGLING FATHER

It would be tempting to end each chapter with Art's words. You the reader can then declare that I am the spiritual superman that everyone should emulate.

But that is not who I am.

I am a husband, a friend, a teacher, a leader, and a father who has been inconsistent far too often in my spiritual role modeling. And more than anyone else, my sons have seen this inconsistency. While Art is kind and God is gracious, I am much weaker spiritually than his story indicates.

But let me tell you what Art's words have done. They have given me a new determination in God's power to be a better spiritual leader than I have been.

To spend more time in God's Word.

To have a more consistent prayer life.

To love others more freely.

To evangelize more regularly.

They may be grown men, but my sons still look to their father as an example for spiritual leadership.

I will do better.

Someone is watching.

Chapter 3

When a Man Loves a Woman

The winter of 2004—2005 was a roller coaster of emotions and heartaches for the Rainer family. It held moments of intense sadness, joy, anticipation, weariness, stress, fear, and everything in between and on every extreme.

We were up, and we were down.

We felt tossed and thrown like rag dolls.

We learned that there were more important things in life than just our daily activities, and we gained a greater understanding of what family and relationships was all about.

That winter my mother, Nellie Jo Rainer, was diagnosed with breast cancer.

And as I am sure many of you understand, the range of emotions experienced during those moments is too complicated and confusing to be put easily into words. My dad, brothers, and I felt as if a grand piano had been put on our backs and we were forced to carry it. Even as I write this, my thoughts are filled with grave concern for my mother, who has just finished her chemotherapy sessions and is starting her radiation therapy. Though I know she hates for me to say this, I still fear what the future might hold.

After all, she is my mom—the love of my father's life.

<hr />

As I arrived at the hospital, the time was getting close for my mom to go into her second cancer surgery. From the previous surgery's test results, the doctors had found that the cancer had spread into her lymph nodes, requiring another operation.

It wasn't even supposed to be cancer, I remember thinking as I walked through the cold hospital halls.

My mom had seemed to beat the odds every time, but the steady diet of bad news made me less certain of what was about to follow.

I walked through the hospital's reception and waiting room into the preoperative area of the building. My girlfriend (now my wife), Sarah, was with me. She had faithfully been there for my tears, confusion, and anger ever since we found out that the cancer had spread beyond the supposedly contained area. She was the one who could bring a smile to my mother's face when we boys could not.

I turned the corner. I could see my mom lying in the hospital bed, and my dad sitting beside his wife, holding her hand. My mom was strong and in good spirits, as she had been since she learned of her cancer. She was a true woman of God and held her faith close as she had always done.

My dad was evidently worried.

The look on my father's face at that moment will be forever engraved in my mind. Never had I seen so much fear and concern in his eyes. His face was blank from the multitude of rushing thoughts that passed through his mind. He was silent, obviously holding back the emotions that yearned to come out but could not be expressed because he did not want to cause my mother any more concern. At that moment I was faced with a possible reality.

We said our good-byes, and my mom was wheeled to surgery.

I pulled Sarah aside, a lump in my throat and tears forming in my eyes. "I can't imagine my father without her. What would he do? She is the love of his life, and so much of him is *her*. Sarah, they just *can't* be separated. They need each other. Wife, friend, confidant: every type of relationship for him is in her."

Sarah held me as I could no longer hold back my tears. I now feared not only for my mother but for my father as well.

WHAT IT TAKES TO BE A HUSBAND

My father has had an incredible relationship with my mother, and in this day and age, there are not many children who can say that. When I say "incredible," I mean that I could not imagine a more God-given relationship than the one that my parents have. Yes, I know this is a little biased, and I am sure that there are other marriages out there that God has evidently blessed, but I will write of the one that has influenced me the most.

I have been very fortunate to witness their relationship, and the lessons I have learned from my father have been and will be priceless for me in my own marriage. As I have expressed repeatedly, the way we children view our parents significantly impacts the decisions we make later down the road.

Let me run through some lessons about marriage that I learned from my father.

The Commitment of a Husband

The world speaks: "Do you really think that I can stay with *one* person the rest of my life? I mean, I would like to, but let's face it, it is highly unlikely. Things happen. People change. Life goes on. As you sit in your dream world where everyone lives happily ever after, I will stay right here in reality. Good luck. I hope you are not too disappointed if you are not part of the minority."

As divorce continues to attack our culture like a spreading disease, infecting all of society, the world has somehow developed a mind-set that the discarding of a marriage is normal, expected, and justifiable. Our society, our world, is giving up on marriage. The sanctity, the holiness of the union between man and woman is crumbling right before us at an alarming rate. It is a crisis. It is dangerous.

I grew up in a home where there was no question as to whether or not my parents would stay together. In fact, most families that we were acquainted with were the same way, and in retrospect, the perspective of marriage to which I grew accustomed is somewhat rare in today's world.

Sure, my parents had disagreements and got into arguments as couples do in any relationship, but even during the most bitter of fights, I never heard my father threaten to leave my mom. Actually, I don't remember my dad remotely coming close to saying that he would separate from my mom, even in a joking manner. I was never given the opportunity to think anything less than my parents' relationship lasting forever.

Dad understood the implications and seriousness of divorce. I believe that he was unwilling to mention divorce with my mom in a passing manner. I see marriages come and go, and I am bombarded with the world's suggestion that divorce is understood, even applauded. But I cannot imagine me doing anything else but being with my wife "till death do us part."

The Romance of a Husband

Whether I liked it or not when I was younger, I had to face the reality that my dad was in love with my mom. I can recall sitting in church, listening to my dad preach, and anytime he mentioned my mom, he had to tell the congregation that he thought that my mom was attractive. He liked to refer to her as a "foxy chick." It must have been some phrase that he picked up in the '60s that was at one time accepted. I hope it was accepted. Poor mom.

Now, many of you may not consider "foxy chick" really romantic, but my father occasionally did the whole flowers-and-gifts thing as well. It's just not as fun to write about. I have never once heard my mother say that my dad was unromantic or complain about the treatment she received from him. My dad has always enjoyed making my mom feel beautiful and loved. His behavior is the outgrowth of his long-term view of the marriage commitment.

My dad knows that he only has one opportunity to get things right for my mom.

There is no do-over.

My wife likes to recall the recent time when we were at a restaurant with my parents, and during the course of the meal, my dad reached under the table to pinch my mom's rear. (I bet this is a side of Dr. Rainer that you didn't expect to hear.) My mom let out a light "Oh!" and smiled at my father.

My wife, not knowing how to react, did not say anything about this until the meal was over and we were heading back home in my car. "I hope that you will pinch my rear when we've been married for that long," Sarah said.

Saying the first thing that came to mind, I looked over at her and said, "Me too."

The Respect of a Husband

One of the rules I most vividly remember from my upbringing was: *"Thou shalt not disobey thy mother, for in doing so thou shalt hear from thy father."*

OK, maybe it wasn't in so much those words, but there is one thing that my brothers and I understood: our dad had our mom's back. Anytime my mom laid down a rule or a punishment, there was no question as to whether or not my dad would agree. It was automatic. My father respected the decisions made by my mother. There was no argument.

Also, my dad respected my mom as a person. Never did it appear that he looked down upon her for anything. Actually, it looked to be the opposite; my dad put her on a pedestal, treating her like the princess that she is. He was very biblical, treating her with the same love that Christ has for the church, willing to lay down his life for her.

Because of these things, I not only view my mom in the same light as did my father, but I respect all women in that manner. In light of the unbiblical perspectives of women today that our culture promotes, it is easy to see why many males lack respect for women.

Even as the message of equality among sexes is continuously preached by our social leaders, there is a stark contrast between that message and the portrayal of women on our televisions, billboards, and magazines. But we can fight. Hope still remains. These images can be made right in the minds of children through the proper treatment of their mother in the home. Greater than television, greater than movies, is the example set at home.

The Care of a Husband

"When Mama's happy, everyone's happy!"

This phrase is primarily used in a joking manner, even though there is some undeniable truth behind it. I am going to switch it up a little to fit my parents' relationship.

"When Mama's happy, Dad is happy."

This seems a little more accurate. You see, my dad seemed to care more about my mother than anything or anybody else except his relationship with God. He was willing to do anything for her to the point where, at times, it seemed to almost consume him. Knowing that my mom would never take advantage of him, my dad would do anything that my mom asked of him.

He would even do some things that he, as a male, didn't understand. Any need, any desire, any request, he would take care of her. He was her servant.

The Friendship of a Husband

My dad and mom are best friends. They love to be around each other and miss each other's company when they are apart. It is a devoted friendship that has taken many years to develop, and it has a deepness that I desire for my wife and myself.

I remember when my younger brother, Jess, graduated high school. Dad frequently traveled for various speaking and consulting engagements around the nation, and the upcoming summer was to be especially busy for him. My mom made the decision to stay home for most of those trips to be with Jess before he headed off to college.

Even though he would miss Jess living at home, Dad excitedly anticipated the day when Mom could start traveling with him. My dad missed her. They had developed such a tight friendship that he felt incomplete without her. He wanted her sitting next to him on each flight. He was very verbal about this, so when the time came for my mom to be able to travel, she was on the next flight. Since then, my parents have traveled the nation together, spending time and enjoying each other's friendship.

No one can really question my parents' companionship. All one needs to do is to sit at the dinner table and listen to them attempt to crack jokes. They tell each other everything, sharing intimate secrets. They know one another inside and out. My dad and mom have reached the level of intimacy that couples should aspire to obtain. Above any man or woman, my dad's friendship with his wife comes first.

Above All, Love

These few areas that I have briefly touched on all revolve around one key factor: love.

The love my dad has for his wife is deep.

When I look at my father, I see a biblical picture of how a husband should love his wife. It seems almost absurd that I can say that I know, without hesitation, that my father would lay down his life for my mom if needed, just as Christ did for us. Am I really comparing my earthly father to my heavenly Father?

In one respect, yes, I am.

The love that my father has for my mom goes well beyond a fuzzy feeling that everyone gets when they first meet someone to whom they are attracted. He made a choice at the altar in a small church in rural Alabama punctuated by an "I do." That decision has stood the tests and trials of time even when the feelings, on which so much of our world relies, seemed to have faded.

It is a love deepened and refined by fire.

What does this do for me? It allows me to see the reality of true marriage. Because I was able to observe such a solid, biblical marriage, I better understand the effort and sacrifice it takes to achieve a deep and lasting bond with my own wife.

I am not naïve as to the work that is required in order to have the relationship that everyone so desires. I understand that someday the infatuation with my wife will run its course and the real marriage will begin. Even though I know there will be struggles, I am better prepared for the journey ahead of me.

I want my wife to be the one and only, and I thank my dad for showing me the way to realize this type of marriage.

— A Father's Perspective —

The first thundering diagnosis: breast cancer. Surgery quickly thereafter. The second and even more cruel telephone call: the cancer had spread to a sentinel lymph node. Second surgery to remove the remaining lymph nodes. Finally good news: no further spread to other lymph nodes. Then the hell called chemotherapy for four months. Then thirty-three radiation treatments.

The sickness. The despair. The shopping for a wig. The hair falling out. The countless trips to the doctors.

Art recalled well the difficult days of that gray winter. Indeed, we had an entire year consumed with the reality of cancer, treatments, and recovery. We are now on the other side. The prognosis is good. God is good.

I learned so much on this road not previously traveled. I learned an even deeper love for a wife I did not know I could love any deeper. I learned the sustaining grace of our Lord. And I learned how much my boys loved this woman who is my wife and who is their mother.

A Not-So-Perfect Husband

The scariest thing about being a husband and a father is the constant awareness that your children are watching you be a husband to their mother. The scrutiny is inescapable.

My boys have seen me lose my temper on too many occasions. Though my wife and I tried to keep our disagreements out of the hearing of our boys, we weren't always successful. And my boys saw a dad who sometimes got mad at their mom.

I am by nature a hard worker. On the one hand, such a trait is commendable. Slothfulness was something my three sons did not see in their dad. On the other hand, an industrious spirit unchecked can become workaholism. I shudder to think how many times my wife took care of the boys when I was supposed to be there.

Even to this day, I admonish my grown sons for working too hard, for not sleeping enough, and for not slowing down and enjoying life more. They give me that knowing smile that says the unspoken words, "I've grown up just like you, Dad. I've grown up just like you."

Too many times my boys saw me help a church member or go to yet another speaking engagement when I should have been there with them and their mother. And in this (hopefully) more mature phase of my life, I realize that I was not nearly as indispensable as I once thought.

But a Husband Who Loves His Wife

I cannot read the first part of this chapter without crying. Art's words bring back powerful emotions of pain, of worry, and of love. I, too, recall the scene he described so vividly: Nellie Jo facing her second surgery, and the unknown of the immediate future as issues of life and death faced both of us. And I recall Art and Sarah coming into the pre-op area.

Art read me well.

He did see intense pain and worry on my face.

And he did see a deep, deep love for the lady who is my wife, the one he calls Mom.

There has been one unmistakable reality in the Rainer home: Thom Rainer loves Nellie Jo Rainer. Despite my bouts of temper, despite my absences from the home, and despite my often workaholic tendencies, my sons knew one fact very clearly. Their dad loves their mom.

Recently two men from LifeWay shared a visit in my home when all three boys were present to be with us. They interviewed the boys and spent a considerable amount of time with them for a project on me. When it was all said and done they said, with due respect, that they were much more impressed with my boys than they were with me.

Now since they are in my employ, they didn't exactly phrase it that way, but I knew what they were saying.

One of the young men from LifeWay said, "Dr. Rainer, I have young children at home. Can you tell me what you did to raise these boys to be the great young men they are today?"

I was absolutely truthful in my curt response, "Marry well." I knew that so much of their character had been shaped by the godly and selfless love of their mother. But as I reflected more on the question, I think now I would give a more complete response.

First, I would say, love Christ. If your children see the love you have for the Savior, they will likely seek that same love themselves.

Second, love your wife. I have made it clear in this book that I have fallen short of being a great dad so often that I am saddened by many of my own recollections. But there has been one clear and unmistakable message I have communicated: I love my wife with all my heart.

My boys have seen this love despite my failures.

My boys have witnessed the consistency of this reality.

My boys know I love their mother.

And my boys have desired to marry women whom they can love and give of themselves with that same devotion.

Now, I could add many other factors to raising children. I could mention encouraging your children constantly. I could note how having fun builds great families. But Art is covering all these issues as he reflects on *Raising Dad*.

I simply want to be redundant at this point. I can think of few things more powerfully positive in raising children as a husband who loves his wife. Those eyes *are* watching, and they are learning from what we do . . . or don't do.

AND THE TWO SHALL BECOME ONE

Art is wise beyond his years. He recognized the powerful message parents communicate when they are united in spirit. The "oneness factor" of marriage has always seemed self-evident to me. Husband and wife are one physically, emotionally, and spiritually.

But I guess I never saw how that oneness issue works in the raising of kids until I had children. Do you remember how Art phrased it? He said Dad "had Mom's back."

He was right. Our sons rarely heard us debate with one another on issues of discipline, curfews, or parameters. Most of the time Nellie Jo and I agreed with each other on the decisions on child rearing. But on those few occasions when we were not of the same mind, we typically took those disagreements behind closed doors until we came to a resolution.

Then we would present a united front once again. Those boys just could not play one parent against the other.

I have to admit something at this point. Nellie Jo has always been a better parent than I have been. I do not make the statement out of false modesty; it is just a reality I accepted.

Frankly, when we had those private disagreements, we usually settled on her perspective. Her selfless maternal instincts nearly always trumped my logical and methodical plans for dealing with our sons.

Now, don't read me wrong. My wife willingly followed my lead in life. She married a banker and became a pastor's wife, a dean's wife, and a president's wife. She was the stable force in our family when we moved from Atlanta to Anniston, from Anniston to Louisville, from Louisville to Madison, from Madison back to Louisville, from Louisville to St. Petersburg, from St. Petersburg to Birmingham, from Birmingham to Louisville, and from Louisville to Nashville.

She followed as I led in the disrupting times in our family's life.

But her willingness to follow does not mean that she has less insight and wisdom. Indeed, she was most often the wiser of the two parents. So in our attempts to present a united front to our sons, I typically yielded to her wisdom.

At least on those occasions, I was a smart man.

AND THE LOVE GROWS

The year began with cancer, surgeries, chemotherapy, and radiation. It concluded with recovery and a good prognosis, a new ministry at LifeWay in Nashville, and a fiftieth birthday celebration for Nellie Jo.

I had in mind two major ways I wanted to celebrate her birthday. First, I would have a dinner party with some of our closest friends. Second, I would propose to her again. I would ask her to "marry" me for the next phase of our lives. And I would buy her a new engagement ring.

Now, the issue of the new engagement ring is a story itself. When I first proposed to Nellie Jo in 1977, I was a person of little financial means. The ring I bought her was relatively small. Years later, while attending to the affairs of our household as she always did so faithfully, she fell down the steps to the garage. She not only broke her foot, she cracked her engagement diamond when her hand hit the concrete with a mighty impact.

Nellie Jo never complained about her ring. She rarely spoke of the crack in the diamond. And she never coveted others who had bigger and more spectacular rings.

But that ring just broke my heart.

She deserved so much more.

It was not a matter of money or the size of the diamond. It was just that she deserved so much more.

So a few days shy of her fiftieth birthday, I emptied my savings account and bought her a new ring.

I gave her that ring in the form of a proposal on the beaches of Cape San Blas, Florida. With the stars glistening in a beautiful and unobstructed sky, I asked my wife of twenty-eight years to marry me again.

She didn't see it coming.

The surprise really worked.

What a great and joy-filled evening!

Before the evening was over, I did what I told myself I wouldn't do: I cried. The emotions overflowed out of control, even if for a few brief moments.

You see, I love my wife so very much. She is the most incredible woman in the world. From the first time I saw her when she was fifteen to the beauty she is at fifty, I have always loved her.

I guess that is what Art, Sam, and Jess saw throughout the years when they saw me look at their mother. I guess they saw through all of my weaknesses and shortcomings and saw how incredibly much I love that girl.

Love your wife.

Your kids will see that as one of the greatest gifts they could ever receive.

Chapter 4

Three Gifts: Support, Encouragement, and Pride

Much of my early childhood, from third to sixth grade, was spent in Alabama. As with any of our moves, my father had been called to pastor one of the local churches. Residing in this state was great for my parents since most of their relatives lived in Alabama at the time, and both of them considered the state their home.

As anyone who grows up in Alabama knows, football is king. It is *the* sport in the state; anything else is considered just an activity. Baseball and basketball? Activities to pass the time until football season begins. And because of this fanatical influence, I am still affected today. For example, I cheer more and get more excited about my alma mater the University of

Kentucky's football team than the basketball team! I know: I am a rare breed. If you know anything about Kentucky, the basketball tradition is one of the richest in the nation, and though the football fans are loyal, they do not compare to the basketball fans. Even after spending more than a decade in Kentucky, I still get more enthused about football than basketball. I can't seem to get enough of the game. (Note: I have made great strides in Football Fanatics Anonymous, otherwise known as FFA. Keep me in your prayers.)

Like most children growing up in Alabama, I had a dream to play the glorious pastime of football. I had listened to my dad tell about his football glory days and wanted to be able to have the same incredible, life-altering experiences that he did. However, this desire was inhibited by two primary factors: my school and my mom.

You see, since I attended a small Christian school, it did not have a football team on which I could play. And even though there were Little League teams I could join, my mother refused to let me play. She feared that one of her boys would get seriously injured, which I felt was a dumb reason at the time.

I remember one day when I was coming home with my dad from church. It was a weekday, and I had probably just hung out at the church after school until he was ready to leave. As we rode home, we took the same route we always did. This route led through the local neighborhood, past the same houses and past the same Little League football field upon which I desired to play.

That day the team was practicing on the field. I looked out the car window to see the team in their colors, black and orange, running around the field. The team name was the Raiders, and, oh, how I longed to be one. Like an ugly puppy that nobody wants to adopt, I looked out the window with a sad, sad yearning and said, "Dad, why won't Mom let me play football?"

"She couldn't bear to see you get hurt," my father responded.

"But I want to play so badly."

"I know, son, just keep holding on to your dreams."

And I did. As time went by, my dad and I would continue to have conversations about playing football one day. He knew that it was a dream of mine, one that I would not let go. He understood and encouraged me to hold on to that dream as long as it did not conflict with my mom's desires.

My dream finally became a reality while I was living in Kentucky. When I was a sophomore in high school, a couple of my friends, who also shared the same desire to play football, and I approached our principal about establishing a team. High school would come to an end in a few years, and we realized that our window of opportunity to play the game was quickly closing up. We brought with us a petition signed by numerous students wanting to have a football team included in our school's athletic program. Surprisingly, the principal agreed, and the next year I was living out my dream.

I am not sure how my mom was able to change her mind about the sport, but I see it as an answer to prayer. She gave me the thumbs up to play, and I took full advantage of the opportunity. I assume that my father was just as excited as I was. He had known my yearning from when I was little and had seen me quench the desire. I attribute so much of the fulfillment of the dream to my father. He gave me the support and encouragement needed and would not let me allow the dream to fall to the wayside. Had he discouraged my desire, I probably would not have continued to seek out the possibility of one day playing. And after the first game, you know who I wanted to talk to afterwards.

Now we *both* have our football stories to tell.

BEING THERE

Whether my interest of the week was football, the guitar, cars, basketball, the French horn, cross country, track, girls (OK, so girls were a little bit more than an interest of the week), baseball cards, fishing, writing, surfing, fraternity life, snowboarding, traveling, or any of the other activities that have held my attention for a short period of time, my father was there.

Whether I wanted to become a neurosurgeon, pilot, preacher, businessman, professional athlete, writer, or rock star, my dad was there. And whether my dreams and aspirations for my future and present would endure or would change twice within the same day, my father was there as well.

Like many American children, I was bombarded with a multitude of opportunities and activities from which to choose, and I wanted to try them all. Anything that seemed new and exciting, I wanted to attempt it. I loved, and still do love, the adventure of learning something that was previously unknown or seemed to be a mystery to me. My favorite activity is when I am doing something that I have never done before.

Granted, my pursuits in all of these activities and goals have given me a wide variety of somewhat random experiences. But they have contributed to the uniqueness of who I am today. And as with any parent whose child's pursuits are constantly changing, I imagine it was difficult for my father to keep up with who I wanted to be. Who I was on one day would change the next. Was Art going to be the football player, surfer, or businessman today? Who knew? Sometimes, I don't even think that I knew or cared. I was just enjoying the adventure of life.

Looking back on the way my father handled me, it seems that all of these changes never really mattered to him. Not that he didn't care what my interests were; he actually cared very much. My dad simply did not seem to concern himself with how often I changed my mind on interests or pursuits.

He was just there for me no matter what.

Through everything that I did, unless it contradicted the Bible, he was there to support, encourage, and take pride in me and all my pursuits.

Support

Support is powerful. It can provide a child with the courage and willingness to pursue goals or accomplish tasks that he or she would otherwise feel were beyond reach. True support can be seen not only from parent to child, but it can be found from boss to employee or teacher to student.

Could a person become president without the backing of the political party? Could a missionary travel to the other side of the globe and be as effective without some type of support system in his or her homeland? Could I have written this book without the support of my father and family? While we can accomplish some on our own without support, it pales in comparison to what we can do when we know that we have backing, whether financially or verbally, to our cause.

That is what my father did for me. Anything that I desired to do in life, he was there supporting me. Any direction that I wanted to go, I had his backing. And I quickly came to understand this even as a child. I knew that I had my father's support on anything. Any decision that I made, I could count on him being there, giving me the foundational backing that I needed.

I never worried about his support.

I always had it.

I did not realize how having this type of support would affect my future, and I had no idea how many children do not receive this support until I had moved away from the home. Because of the backing that I received while growing up, I have great confidence in myself, my ideas, and the personal goals that I feel are placed before me. I am not saying that all of my ideas are amazing, or that all of my goals have been met, but I remain unafraid to pursue, unafraid to reach, unafraid to live the life that God desires for me to experience.

It's funny: even though I have been gone from the home for quite a while now, I still feel that I have my dad's support surrounding me. I am finding that what my father did for me while I was younger has now carried over into my adulthood. Even though he may have no clue what my next move may be, I feel that I have his support. It gives me the courage needed to pursue and accomplish whatever might be laid on my heart.

Encouragement

Because encouragement and support seem similar at first glance, let me explain the difference. Support, as I explained, is the backing that you receive from someone. Encouragement is taking support one step further. It includes a push to proceed.

My father is one of the greatest encouragers in my life. Anytime I came to him with an idea or decision, he would push me to continue in that direction. He would continually ask me about that idea or decision until I decided that I no longer wanted to pursue it. He made sure that I was the one who made the decision whether or not to follow an idea.

When things went well, whether it was a win at a baseball game, a wave caught surfing, or a good grade received on a paper, he was one of the first to congratulate me. And when things went wrong, he was one of the first to pat my back and tell me that everything was going to be fine.

And in between these times, he was there constantly encouraging me until the end.

Pride

Even as I get older, I have yet to grow weary of hearing about my father's pride in me. It is special, and I cherish each time. I loved it when I was young, and I still love it now when I hear his coworkers tell of how my dad was bragging about me to others. Many of these compliments I feel are undeserved, but I take pleasure in hearing them nonetheless. The fact that I know my father is proud of me means more to me than he will ever know.

I have yet to meet a child who did not long for the gift of pride from his or her parents. There is just something about hearing your parents say that they are proud of you or hearing them talk well of you to their friends that makes you stick out your chest and hold your head high. Even when I was a boy, I felt like a man when I knew that my dad was proud of me. You know that you have done something right and are being recognized for your actions. Many children continuously seek the approval of their parents and never receive it, and this lack of encouragement can follow the child into his or her adulthood.

I appreciate that my father is not afraid or hesitant to verbally tell my brothers and me that he is proud of us. He has always been this way and has been telling us of his pride for as long as I can remember.

By my father telling me that he was proud of me, I was encouraged in whatever I did. I do not know of anyone who would not like to hear that someone is proud of them. It puts confidence in that person to continue on the path, pursuing their goal, and reach for what once seemed unattainable. If it hadn't been for my father's pride in me, there would have been a void or a desire that would not have been fulfilled. Sadly, many of my peers tell me that, even as adults, they are still trying to get their father's approval. Fruitlessly, they continue to try to fill a void that has existed since childhood.

I cannot imagine where my life would be without the support, encouragement, and pride of my father. Those factors had such a tremendous impact on my life that I know I would be a different person from who I am today if I had not received them.

I am fortunate to have experienced these three gifts of parenting—support, encouragement, and pride—from my father because I know that many children have not.

I hope that I am able to give these same gifts to my children someday.

Who knows? Maybe I will be sitting around exchanging football stories with my children one day.

And the gift goes on.

— *A Father's Perspective* —

I knew my father was proud of me.

I just wish he had told me that a bit more than he did.

When I was twelve years old, he gave me a job at the small-town bank where he was president. I know that he was proud to see his son carrying on the multigenerational tradition of banking. And I know he was exceedingly proud when I accepted a job in an Atlanta bank in their management training program. And the day I was promoted to vice president at age twenty-six was a day I saw great pride in his face.

I just wish he had told me a bit more than he did.

Like most children, I longed for the approval of my parents, and my father in particular. And though I never doubted his approval and love, his quiet and reticent ways left me yearning to hear from him verbally.

I cannot recall having an intentional plan to verbalize my approval to my sons. I do remember well the great excitement I would have about being a father one day, even when I was just a kid myself.

And I guess I was just determined to make certain my sons knew the great joy I had in them.

WHEN A FATHER SUPPORTS HIS SON

Art makes it seem like my support for him flowed as easily as a downhill stream. On the one hand, he is absolutely right. I have such incredible joy in my three boys that my support of them is as natural as it can be. On the other hand, there have been times when I have been totally perplexed as to exactly how to support my sons.

One of my biggest struggles was their relationships with girlfriends.

One of my sons, around sixteen years old at the time, had just concluded a lengthy telephone conversation with his girlfriend. I could sense something was wrong, and my intuition was supported by the fact that he did not come out of his bedroom.

I knocked on his bedroom door and got no answer. When I entered the room, I saw him with his pillow over his head, attempting to muffle the anguish he felt. The relationship had ended.

As I sat on the edge of the bed, my son told me in no uncertain terms that I should leave the room. My pleas for conversation were met with even greater anger and pain. I left quietly, offering the simple words, "I am here for you, son, if you need me."

There was so much I needed to learn about being a parent. No books or classes, though, could fully prepare me for girlfriends, cruel friends, and bad coaches.

Another of my sons had a coach who constantly berated and yelled at his players. His booming voice could be heard by everyone, home fans and visitors alike. In an effort to support my son, I decided to have a conversation with this coach. I soon learned that I had "ruined my son's life" by having that conversation. From his perspective, any conversation I had with that coach jeopardized his status on the team and embarrassed him in front of his peers. Did I make a mistake by supporting my son in this manner?

By the way, in the years that have followed, many parents and former players have affirmed my decision. It's just tough to know sometimes how to demonstrate this support.

One thing I do know, however: all children yearn to know that they have the support of their parents. Fathers, please hear me well. Your children want to know of your love *and* support. And we cannot assume they know of that support unless we articulate it.

THAT ENCOURAGEMENT THING

I like Art's definition of encouragement: a push to proceed. My father rarely verbalized his encouragement of me, though I knew he was proud of me. But my mother was a different story. When Mama would express her belief in me, something that was a regular occurrence in person or by phone, I really believed that I could conquer the world.

My wife and I have never been reticent to encourage our sons. Indeed, if I may speak in light of my own fallibility, I would exhort, encourage, and plead with fathers to be a constant source of encouragement for their children. I believe as Art does that encouragement played a major role in the confidence and strength all three of my sons demonstrate today.

One area with which I struggled was the balance of encouragement and discipline. Later in this book Art tells the story of his "kidnapping" of a fellow student while he was in high school. It was a not-so-bright prank by Art and a couple of friends who were avenging another friend whose house had been "TP'd" (covered with toilet paper).

I was mad at everybody when I got the call to come to the school. I was mad at Art for the dumb prank. I was mad at his co-conspirator friends. I was mad at the parents of the "kidnapped" boy, because they saw nothing wrong in what their precious and perfect son had done in TPing the house. I was mad at the principal of the school who seemed more concerned about a lawsuit than doing the right thing.

I have to change the subject quickly because I am getting mad retelling an old story.

The years have passed and I have forgotten many of the details of that unfortunate day. I do remember my anger, and I do remember I punished Art, but I cannot recall the nature of the punishment.

But the most vivid memory of that incident was my own struggles on *how* to punish Art. I wanted him to be contrite for his wrongdoing, but I did not want to break his spirit.

I remember the first time I had those inner struggles. Sam, our oldest son, had just begun to walk. He had stern warnings from me not to touch the vase on the coffee table. After three warnings, Sam still touched the vase. I grabbed the little hand of my son and popped it with my own hand.

I still remember the look on his face today.

Sam seemed to be in shock for about five seconds. *Did my daddy really do that?* Then he began to cry convulsively. Even though the pop to the hand was light, I still have guilt about that moment. When does discipline discourage a child?

Children need encouragement, whether they are five or fifty years old.

I am a fifty-one-year-old man, and I have seen many changes in my life. But one thing remains unchanged: People need hope and encouragement, especially from those closest to them.

The man in my office was about my age. I am not sure how we moved to the subject, but he began to tell me about his elderly father. "I have been chasing my father's approval all my life. It seems I just can't measure up for him," my friend said sadly. "I long for his blessing, but he always tells me how I could do better."

The next week would prove particularly difficult for my friend. "I have to move Dad out of the home where he has lived for over forty years," he said quietly. "I dread the pain I will see on Dad's face when I tell him that he can't live in his own home anymore. I dread the hurt that this will cause him."

Tears welled in my friend's eyes. "But you know what I dread the most?" he asked, not expecting an answer. I already knew what he would say. "I am sick to my stomach anticipating how Dad will berate me, how he will tell me how I am letting him down again. I just wish for once that Dad will tell me that he is proud of me. I want his blessing so much."

The blessing. Our children just want to know that we are proud of them.

THE GOOD KIND OF PRIDE

Self pride is haughty and sinful. But pride in a child can be healthy, if not life changing.

———————————

My father was dying.

Even today, years later, those words are difficult to write. He was my hero, my role model, and my best friend.

At age sixty-two, he was just too young to die. He had to see his grandchildren grow up. He had to see me progress in life. He had to get to know my wife, his daughter-in-law, better.

But he was dying.

As I sat by his bedside, I had difficulty expressing myself. You see, Dad and I always had a great relationship, except we just did not talk in depth. He was a quiet man, and I am not the most loquacious person myself.

On that day, which would prove to be the next-to-last day he was able to communicate with me, I wanted to know if he was proud of me. While he had never given me reason to believe otherwise, he really had not demonstrated much pride in me.

I had this fear that I had disappointed him. I broke the multigenerational chain of bankers in my family to become the first to enter vocational ministry. He had always been so proud of my banking accomplishments, but he just did not seem to have that same glow when I talked about my new adventures in ministry training at seminary.

Perhaps he saw the look on my face.

Or maybe God gave him insight to my moments of doubt.

In either case, he looked up from his pillow and painfully moved his body to sit up a bit. He looked me straight in the eyes. His own eyes were filled with tears.

"I am so proud of you, son."

That did it.

I could let Dad go now.

He *was* proud of me.

———

Art and his brothers should never doubt my healthy pride in them. In fact, I find it difficult not to talk about my boys wherever I go and in whatever venue I find myself. They are the joy and pride of my life.

I have done many things wrong as a father. I have traveled too much. I have been short-tempered. And I have put work before family.

But I have always been proud of my sons. And they know it.

And I have to believe that one of the key reasons they have grown up to be such fine men is that they have always known that my wife and I are proud of them. They have that confidence and assurance.

We parents can indulge our children with material gifts without ceasing. We can give them money indiscriminately. We can send them to the finest schools. And we can pay for their travels to endless places.

But all children need more. They need the gifts of support, encouragement, and pride. Without these gifts, everything else we give them is of little value. They simply need to know that they are valued.

Art has very few memories of my father. Indeed, I have few memories of Art and my dad together because Art was so young when Dad died.

But there was one moment I will treasure all my life.

My dad had Art in his lap as he attempted to teach my toddler son the names of his grandparents. My father pointed to himself and said, "Daddy Man."

Art grinned knowingly.

Dad then pointed to my mother and said, "Nana."

Art grinned again.

My parents waited a few seconds to see if Art understood. My son seemed to have a burst of awareness, and pointed to his own chest and yelled out, "Art!"

Both my mom and dad began to roar in convulsive laughter.

When my father regained his composure, he wiped the tears of laughter from his eyes. Dad beamed with a pride that I had rarely seen. "This boy," he declared, "is just like his daddy."

Perhaps one day soon I will have a grandchild in my lap. And perhaps I will declare the same pride for that child that I did for his or her father.

My father was proud of me.

I am proud of Art.

And Art will beam with pride at his first child.

And the gift goes on.

Chapter 5

The Lost Art of Discipline

No matter what high school you attend, there seems to be a pecking order or hierarchy in place that is recognized throughout the student body. Typically the most noticeable rankings are broken down into classes, such as freshman, sophomore, junior, and senior. Being the eldest, the seniors usually have the biggest voice and the most respect among the student body while the freshmen are just that to the rest of the school: little, annoying freshman.

There are also rankings within each class, ranging from those who are the "coolest" to those who are considered "losers." And whether or not any school officials, especially at the Christian school that I attended, would actually admit that this occurs among their student population, the fact remains that the popularity contest in high school has and, unfortunately, probably always will exist.

Just ask any student. Being a high school student can be a very confusing and trying time. Everyone has some inclination to be accepted and liked by their peers. Students can do the most incomprehensible things to "earn" their classmates' respect. Now, looking back, it all seems so stupid and pointless.

Shamefully, I must admit that I was one of those students caught up in the pecking order in school, and it resulted in my getting in trouble with both the school and my father. A nasty combination for any child.

It was right before spring break of my junior year in high school. The seniors had left to go on their senior class trip, leaving us as the "big guys" on campus for a week. For whatever reason, we felt a sense of pride and arrogance.

Unbeknownst to us, this newfound pride we had just received was about to receive a setback. Early Monday morning, my group of guy friends and I got word that Cameron (one of our closest friends in the group) had just gotten his house rolled (toilet papered). And it wasn't just the fact that his house was rolled that made us mad, but that the rolling was done by a sophomore! How dare a SOPHOMORE roll a junior's house! Who did this guy think he was? There was absolutely no way that we could let him get away with this. Something had to be done. A message needed to be sent.

Being the geniuses that we were, we took it upon ourselves to make sure he learned his lesson. What did we decide to do? We would kidnap him, take him to Cameron's house, and make him clean up the mess that he had made. Genius.

After school, Cameron, Matt, Adam, Greg, and I immediately went to the school parking lot and hopped in Cameron's SUV. There, we waited for our guy, whom we will call Mike.

When we saw Mike walk out of the school building and head towards his car, we started up the SUV. Slowly, we crept behind him at a safe distance so he would not be aware of the automobile that was following him in the parking lot. Gradually, the distance shortened between us and our target. Then, as he neared his car, the excitement began.

Cameron sped up his SUV to get within closing distance of Mike. He slammed on the brakes and we all jumped out of the vehicle. Running, we caught up with Mike and grabbed him. A struggle ensued between Mike and us as we tried to throw him into Cameron's car.

At this point, Greg bailed. "C'mon guys, I'll clean up the mess!"

"Shut up, Greg!" we said as we finally forced Mike in the automobile. (Greg is now following God's plan for his life as a minister.)

Once Mike was in the SUV, we headed towards Cameron's house. Mike was being held down by Matt and me in the backseat of the automobile. I had his legs and Matt had his head.

We did not make it to Cameron's house because never before had we seen anyone so scared in all of our lives. It caught us off guard. Mike acted as if he were about to be killed. His face was filled with fear, he was shaking, and he had started to breathe as if hyperventilating. The poor kid was freaking out way more than we had anticipated! We decided our point had been made and justice was done, so nothing further was needed. We turned the SUV around, went back to the school, and let Mike out.

Now this story would be pointless to this chapter unless I said something about the punishment I received.

I was punished by both the school and my parents. For the school, I had to serve detention and do a certain amount of community service. For my parents, my dad was the primary executor of the punishment! I was forced off the track team and was grounded for a couple of weekends. In addition to this, all families involved had to deal with the anger and frustration of Mike's parents, who were obviously very defensive of their son who had been briefly kidnapped. It was a mess. All of this for a stupid act of high school pride.

PUNISHMENT AND THE CRIME

I could actually give you several examples of when my father had to discipline me. Because I had the hottest temper in my family, I had several fallouts with both of my brothers, which always resulted in some form of reprimand. Now I understand that each child and family is different, and punishments must be decided accordingly. Also, I am fully aware that some people view punishments such as spankings as being harmful or abusive to the children. Even though I had to endure spankings, my dad was neither harmful nor abusive, and looking back on the numerous times that I got in trouble, I would not have done anything differently if I were in my father's shoes. Trust me, I needed a few good pops on the rear on more than one occasion.

He Was Not Afraid to Punish

My father was not hesitant to punish his sons. Among my two brothers and me was a lot of pure, high-octane testosterone. We were not always the easiest to handle, especially when competition was involved—and even more so when the competition involved me and my younger brother, Jess. We shared an intense sibling rivalry that resulted in several fights because neither one of us liked to lose to the other. Let me rephrase that: we *hated* losing to the other. I will tell some stories about that later on.

I cannot imagine our home without my dad stepping in to reprimand us boys when we did something wrong. Early on in our lives we learned what was wrong and what was right. When we did something wrong, such as hit one of our brothers, we knew that we were going to pay for that action. There was a definite action/response set in place without fail, because my father did not hesitate to punish us. He did not worry about whether we would love him less if he were to reprimand us.

No, he reprimanded us *because* of his love towards us and not our love towards him.

My dad made sure that we understood that there was a good and a bad, a right and a wrong, and consequences for both.

There Was Purpose Behind the Punishment

Being around several households throughout my childhood, I observed parents punish their children verbally, physically, and by grounding them for no real reason. Most of the time, the parent was in a foul mood and took it out on his or her child. Many times, the kid was just in the wrong place at the wrong time and did little or nothing wrong, and there was no meaningful purpose behind the punishment.

Looking back, I cannot remember a time when I was punished without reason. Normally, there was a lesson to be taught. I had done something wrong and needed to pay the consequences.

When I pushed my younger brother into a piece of furniture, which caused him to slice open his foot, because he was disrupting my view of the television (pretty petty, huh?), I got in trouble. My father grounded me for quite a while to teach me the lesson: Do not push your little brother into furniture. Had I not been reprimanded, I would have been taught a different lesson: It is OK to let your temper flair and get the best of you. Because the punishment always took place after I did something wrong, I never had to question the reasoning behind my punishment.

He Did It with Fairness

Punishments were always fair in our family's household, fitting the crime. With three boys, this is very important. We were always comparing the treatment of one over the other. If Jess and Sam did the exact same thing, just at different times, we compared the consequences for the acts committed. Jess would not let Sam get off easier than he and vice versa.

I believe that the fairness of punishing was very important in my raising. If one reprimand was too severe for what I did and for another situation too light, there could have been a great deal of confusion. The consistency in my punishments gave me benchmarks with which I could measure the severity of my misbehavior.

A United Front

When it comes to parents, children easily learn which parent to go to and for what situation. Generally, there is one parent who is more lenient than the other, and many times, the parents are not on the same page with the reprimands that are in store for the children. Kids use this to their advantage, and my brothers and I were no exception. We realized that our parents were not always fully aware of the punishments that the other had put in place. We used this knowledge to try to manipulate the punishment system and obtain a lighter sentence.

As soon as a punishment had been decreed by one parent, we would seek out the other and woo them by saying things like "I love you" and "You're the best parent in the whole world!" Then, when the punishing parent entered the scene, we would try to make him or her appear too harsh and unjust. Did this ever work? On occasion but not often. Much to our disappointment, most of the time our parents were very good about standing by the other's decision.

My father especially supported my mom's rulings.

I don't know if this was because he was such a great husband or he just didn't want to feel my mom's wrath later! Either way, she had his backing.

Many times my parents convened privately in their room to discuss the appropriate punishment. Those were some of the most nerve-racking times for my brothers and me. We could only sit and wait while trying to overhear the conversation. When they came out, they would present the ruling that was to be upheld.

And if my mom ever wanted her say in what punishment my dad was planning, he would let her give her opinion without hesitation. My father made sure that we realized this was not dad versus mom when deciding our fate, but a mutual agreement from both of them.

He Was Not Too Proud to Rethink His Actions

Although it didn't happen very often, sometimes my father felt that he had given us a punishment that did not fit the crime, and he decided to lighten the load. The primary time this was done was for the duration of our grounding from a particular activity that we enjoyed, such as watching television, hanging out with friends, or going on dates (when we were older). If he felt that the punishment had been too harsh or too long, he would change it to what he felt we rightly deserved.

The Price Had Been Paid Once the Punishment Was Complete

The great thing about being punished when I was younger was that when it ended, the price had been paid. No longer did a cloud of anger or frustration hang over my father. I had learned my lesson and all was well.

I can remember as a young kid running out of my room after being punished to see my father, the man who reprimanded me. I did this because I knew that now, everything was over, and I could go up to him, receive a hug, and let him tell me that he loved me. He did not harbor any bitterness because of my disobedience. He would make sure that I understood why I was punished by quickly going over the situation so that there was no confusion.

After this, I would hang out with my dad a little more or go play with my toys. Either way, I was happy. I did not remain angry or upset because he did not. I would smile and laugh because he would smile and laugh.

I would still love him because I knew that he still loved me.

Sadly, I saw different situations in my peers' homes. Some of my friends were constantly berated by their parents or punished for no apparent reason. They remain insecure to this day.

Others were never punished. Because their parents never demonstrated the true love of discipline, these peers often found themselves in trouble, even in trouble with the law.

But my dad somehow got it right—enough discipline so that I knew right from wrong balanced with enough love and compassion so that I never felt that I was being rejected by him.

Now that I am a married man who plans to have children one day, I hope I learned this balance well.

But I can only hope that my kids aren't nearly as stubborn as I was!

— A Father's Perspective —

Art is right on many counts. He was a stubborn kid. One of our closest friends, Peggy Dutton, often said: "Yep, that middle kid is so much like his father!"

But Art's tenacity is one of his greatest strengths today. My wife and I had to somehow make certain that we directed that stubborn energy to become a positive characteristic for our son. Indeed, all three of our sons are intensely competitive, and that competitive spirit would sometimes lead to disagreements and fights among them.

We wanted to correct their missteps without killing their spirits.

That balance was never easy.

THE BALANCING ACT

As I already mentioned, I will forever be indebted to James Dobson. His books and other resources from Focus on the

Family have been a godsend to this father. But no amount of resources can fully prepare one for the real act of parenting. One area in which I struggle was balancing the level of punishment for the act of disobedience.

Art mentions that Nellie Jo and I were always fair in meting out the punishments to each of the boys. I am not certain that his perspective is totally accurate. Let me explain.

Though I cannot recall specific incidents, I know there were times when Sam, Art, and Jess disobeyed in nearly identical ways. For example, all of them stayed out past their curfew on more than one occasion when they were teenagers. But they did not all receive equal punishments.

Each of our boys responded differently to different types of punishments. For example, if Art and Sam were grounded to their rooms for a day, Sam would be miserable but Art would be just fine. Art had no problem entertaining himself for hours, but Sam was unhappy without an abundance of social interaction.

So the punishments were often unequal because the boys have such different personalities.

Were we wrong not to mete out equal punishments? I still have uncertainties to this day.

One son would need a quick hug to accompany the punishment, while another son needed a period of cooling off before we assured him of our love. Were we wrong to treat them differently? Maybe so, but it seemed like the best path at the time.

Parenting is not easy, and the punishment issue is among the toughest factors to resolve.

And it really gets tough to punish your kids when you have a temper problem yourself.

Yeah, I'm talking about me.

THE HOT-TEMPERED PARENT

For most people who know me at a distance, my public persona is the perception they have of me. I can interact very well with others, and I may seem to have a warmth and sense of humor.

Though I don't think I am a complete ogre, public perceptions don't always match with reality. At heart I am an introvert, and spending time talking to people I hardly know drains my energy. Yes, I can be warm and humorous, but there is a darker side to me as well.

I have a bad temper.

As a child, I dealt with this reality in athletic competition and in encounters with my older brother.

As a parent, I struggled with my temper in the area of discipline. It is an act of grace that Art did not see that in me as often as it really took place.

I could give examples from situations with each of my sons, but this is Art's book, so I will pick on him.

Art often had a problem with tardiness. He simply was not in a hurry as a child, and he sometimes made his entire family late for some function or event.

In 1991, Art was a nine-year-old, and his tardiness was becoming severe. I warned him that the next time he was late for something, he would be punished.

He smiled with a smirk that said, "We'll see."

As expected, the tardy behavior took place less than a day after the warning. While I don't recall where we were going, I do remember clearly that Art was the cause of tardiness. When I began to chastise him, he quickly responded, "I am a child of God, and you have no right to speak to me that way."

I was about to explode! Not only were we late again, but he had spoken to me in a curt and disrespectful manner. I wondered if he had learned that line at the Christian school.

In a show of stubborn wills, I was mad and determined to win. I decided to show Art who was in charge, so I declared with anger that he was grounded from all activities except school and church *for three weeks*. No playing with friends. No baseball games. No television. Nothing. Absolutely nothing. Yeah, take that, you nine-year-old.

Art was devastated. He went to his room and slammed the door.

My wife gave me "the look."

Sam and Jess glowed with the shine of victory.

I walked away mad.

You see, Art does have a revisionist history of how I disciplined him and his brothers. On more occasions than I am comfortable to admit, I punished my boys out of my anger. While I wasn't abusive, I didn't give my sons tough love. I just gave them "tough."

What did I do on those occasions where my flesh did not yield to the Spirit? How did I rectify my wrongdoings? I had to learn to seek forgiveness from my sons.

FROM THE DISCIPLINE OF CHILDREN TO SELF-DISCIPLINE

It usually didn't take me long to realize that I blew it. The look on Art's face haunted me. *Three weeks of grounding. No friends. No television. No baseball.* Yeah, I really blew it. The punishment fit my anger, but not his wrongdoing.

It was time for me to discipline myself instead of discipling my son. When I walked into his room, the look on Art's face was a mix of hurt and anger. I didn't waste time. "Art, I really got too mad at you. I let my anger get the best of me. You don't deserve the punishment I gave you. Will you forgive me?"

Art's disposition changed immediately. I knew that part of his joy was the commuting of his sentence. But I really believe that his greater joy was the result of my changed attitude toward him. Children really do want the approval and unconditional love of their parents.

PUNISHMENT THAT FITS THE CRIME

I also struggled with knowing the severity of the punishment to give to my boys when they disobeyed. It seemed as if my wife, Nellie Jo, was more intuitive in this matter than I, especially when the boys were teenagers.

Sam, our oldest son, was in a foul mood one day. At seventeen, he was sure that he knew more than his ignorant parents. I am not certain what triggered his verbal barrage against us that day, but he was unyielding in his words.

Nellie Jo and I knew that a quick response was in order. My wife quietly said, "Let me handle this."

No argument from me.

Sam was calmly told that he had to turn in his driver's license to his mother for two weeks and, of course, he could not drive. He could only ride with someone when an adult was driving. No exceptions. But he had no other restrictions.

It didn't take my eldest child long to realize the implication of his punishment. One of his parents had to drive him to and from school. And dating. What about dating? Probably the most revealing insight into the severity of his punishment was the evening that his girlfriend picked him up for a date— *with her mother driving!*

I can't recall Sam talking back to us again.

By now you know of the unabashed pride I have in my sons. When I made the punishment to fit the crime, they always responded positively and redemptively. I am indeed proud of their response to their missteps. But when the punishment was excessive and unfair, they knew it. They lost respect for me, at least for a season.

I wish I could say that I had the system down perfectly. I made many mistakes, and I would often be too lenient or too harsh. But my boys had their ways of communicating with me when I missed it. I guess that's what it means to raise Dad.

TOUGH LOVE

I am fully convinced that many parents today are failing to show true love to their children because they are failing to discipline them. The writer of Hebrews articulates how our Father in heaven demonstrates His love through discipline: "My son, do not take the Lord's discipline lightly, or faint when you are reproved by Him; for the Lord disciplines the one He loves, and punishes every son whom He receives" (Heb. 12:5–6). If I am to follow the pattern of my heavenly Father, then I must be willing and desirous to demonstrate my love to Art and his brothers through discipline.

Though I never received a rave review for the disciplinary actions towards my sons when they were younger, I hear frequently today of their desire to emulate my pattern when they have their own children. "Dad," youngest son Jess shared with me not too long ago, "I would get so mad when you punished me. But I sure am glad you loved me enough not to listen to me then."

Tough love is never easy at the time. The easier path is to let the children continue in their disobedience. But the fate that awaits an undisciplined child is rarely good. Tough love is true love, and I thank God that Nellie Jo and I learned that truth in parenting three wonderful sons.

DISCIPLINE: THE NEXT GENERATION

All three of our sons were married in one year's time. We have been blessed with the great gift of daughters-in-law Sarah, Erin, and Rachel. Nellie Jo and I await with great anticipation the advent of grandchildren from these new families.

It will be fascinating to watch how our sons respond to any disobedience evident in their own children. I have a hunch that they will take a path similar to that of Nellie Jo and me. They will discipline their children because they love them.

And how will Nellie Jo and I respond to these new grandchildren coming into our lives? I can almost see this future in my mind's eye. One of our precious grandchildren will be at our home. And perhaps that grandchild will not heed our admonitions despite our repeated warnings.

Will we discipline them as we did their dads? Will we show tough love as we did toward Sam, Art, and Jess?

Nah.

We will spoil them like crazy and let their parents handle the discipline.

OK, I am inconsistent.

But I can't wait for the time to love these grandchildren like crazy. And when they start acting up, a phone call will be in order. "Art [or Sam or Jess], it's time to come get the kids. They need you to discipline them."

Chapter 6

The Family of Fun

It was the summer before my fifth-grade year, and my family was on a vacation in Dallas, Texas. We had seen several sights, such as the Texas Book Depository—the place from which President Kennedy was shot—and we had done several activities, such as dropping down a water slide that left us at an almost vertical free fall before leveling out to the ground. The week had been exciting enough to keep us boys entertained practically nonstop; but as every vacation does, it was coming to an end. Though saddened by the thought of this time concluding, there was still one more day and one more thing to do. The amusement park.

My family loved to go to amusement parks, so I guess you could consider us a somewhat thrill-seeking family. For each of us, there is a desire to ride the fastest, loop the most, and drop from the highest point that we can. We would ride anything that the amusement park offered, enjoying every hill, spin, and twist. But out of all of the rides that day in Dallas, the most memorable comes from the unexpected, the Ferris wheel.

The wheel was huge. You could be seen from almost any point in the park. It towered over almost all of the rides, far larger than you see at any fair. And as we got closer, my brothers and I rallied behind what had become the anthem of the day:

"Can we ride it? Can we ride it? Can we ride it?"

As we jumped up and down with anticipation, my parents agreed to ride the giant wheel.

We went up to the height marker to make sure that we could all ride. My younger brother, Jess, who had just finished the first grade, did not reach the limit. He started crying. My mom, always putting others first, decided to stay back with Jess as my dad, Sam, and I entered the line leading up to the Ferris wheel. Now that we were closer, it seemed to have grown even larger.

The cars on this ride were not like those of a traditional Ferris wheel. The passengers sat on a circular bench inside of the same shaped car. This allowed each rider to have a perfect view of the other passengers in the car. In the middle of the car was a pole that went from the floor of the car to a metal umbrella-like covering above. Like most Ferris wheels, the car was open aired, enabling a great view no matter which way your head was turned. As we gradually moved up to the front of the line, it became our turn to enter into the contraption.

We hopped in the car, and the small aluminum gate was locked behind us. Then we slowly began to rise.

Now as most of you know, the best part of riding the Ferris wheel is when the wheel stops to let others either off or on. This allows those still riding to hang motionless for a brief period of time. And for those few who are extremely lucky, the stop results in their being on top of the Ferris wheel—high above everything and everyone else.

I think it is time to mention one little fact: my dad is scared of heights (now the story gets interesting). Heights do not affect him as long as he is moving. Therefore, the elevation on a ride such as a roller coaster does nothing to him. However, whenever he is stationary, he begins to have serious bouts of acrophobia.

As we were on our fourth round on the Ferris wheel, I think that God began to speak to the conductor of the wheel below and tell him of my father's fear. As we neared the top, the ride began to slow down until it came to a complete stop. There were no cars above us—only the tops of other cars could be seen. Our car was rocking gently as quietness surrounded us; we couldn't even hear the park noises below. We had stopped on the highest point on the ride.

Sam and I loved this, but when we looked at my dad, he didn't show the same excitement. In fact, he had grown a little pale, had a queasy look on his face, and was staring directly at the floor.

"What's wrong, Dad?"

His knuckles turned white as he held tight to the car.

"Nothing, just please sit still."

Sam and I sat there, but as we looked around, we saw something that we had not noticed before. The cars below us were somehow circularly spinning.

Neither of us said a word, but it was obvious what the other had racing through his mind. On the middle pole of the car was what looked like a steering wheel facing upwards. Immediately we grabbed it and started turning it to test out our ability. Before we could even make a full rotation, however, my dad began to speak with urgency.

"Don't you even think about it. If you even turn that thing one more inch, I will hang you upside down by your nostrils!" (A common threat from my dad that would never actually take place.)

Needless to say, we let go, and the Ferris wheel started moving again. As we got off the ride, Sam and I told our mom about getting stuck at the top.

Knowing of my dad's fear, she turned to him, "How did you handle that?"

"Great! Now, if you'll excuse me, I've got to go to the restroom."

And off he went.

———

Perhaps you are asking yourself, *How does your dad freaking out on a Ferris wheel relate to having fun? That does not sound like a good time to me.* It is a reasonable question. All I can say is: You just had to be there. Granted, my father probably was not having fun, but Sam and I were having a blast watching my dad scare himself to death as we sat there, the little brave ones. Whenever my family looks back on that moment, we all have a good laugh (including my dad). Needless to say, I don't think he has been on a Ferris wheel since.

SERIOUS ABOUT FUN

My dad taught me a lot about having fun. Now that may seem an odd lesson to be taught by a parent, but then again, is there anyone who makes more of an impact on a child's life, whether good or bad, than a parent? I watched my dad in almost every aspect of life, including his enjoyment of living.

Anyone who enters the Rainer household soon learns that my dad enjoys his own attempts at humor (notice "attempts") and fun. He has always loved to laugh, tell jokes, and talk of the weirdest things. He is entertainment to whatever "lucky" soul might walk through the door.

Now I understand that everybody has different ways of enjoying life and laughing at it. Some, like my dad, might talk about weird stuff, while others might tell of their latest hiking adventure. This is good. We were meant to have fun during our time here on earth. God gave us the ability to laugh, smile, and enjoy the world He created. There is a time for everything, and my father's time of fun proved to be a great example to me. He seemed to enjoy life in all circumstances. Whether monetarily and physically poor or well off, my dad's perspective on life remained the same.

GOOD, CLEAN FUN

One of the most important reasons why I decided to put this chapter in this book is for this small section you are reading. As stated before, I learned many lessons on fun from my father, and by lessons, I mean how to enjoy myself in a way that would put a smile on God's face. In the Rainer household, the jokes that were told and the activities that were held all seemed done as if Jesus were sitting right there listening and participating.

The phrase "good, clean fun" appears to have a negative stigma attached to it in today's culture. Nothing that is good can be fun, and vice versa. With the bombardment of today's media in all households, it becomes difficult to escape this message. I was susceptible to this in my childhood and, because it continues to intensify, I can only imagine what today's youth are facing. It takes a role model to show them differently, one who is having fun the way God intended us to have it—a more deep and joyous fun than anything this world could offer us. God wants us to have a joyous life, and the best way children can learn it is from the visual example of their parents' pursuit of this same kind of life.

My dad was an incredible picture of how to laugh at things at which Jesus would laugh, do activities that Jesus would do, and enjoy life the way Jesus would enjoy His life. "Good, clean fun" can be found in today's world. Granted, it is not what is most easily accessible, but it is worth the pursuit. I truly believe that more smiles will be made, more laughs will be had, and tighter bonds will be formed than ever before when a family chases after this type of fun. As a kid, one of the best ways that I was able to find this growing up was following my dad's lead.

BE SURE TO ENJOY LIFE

There are many reasons why God put my parents together. One is that they balance each other. My mom is very protective, not wanting to put her children at risk in any way, and my father, well, he is not as cautious. Part of this may stem from his understanding of what it is like to be a boy, to want adventure and risk. Neither one of my parents was wrong, and an argument could be made for each position. However, since this is a book about my father, I will focus on his view.

My dad wanted us to enjoy life. Since he understood what it was like to be a guy, he encouraged us to pursue activities that would fulfill our desires of excitement and exploration. I have mentioned in a previous chapter several of the activities that I have pursued, and many of them have some inherent physical risk to them. However, despite the risk, my dad encouraged me to surf, play football, and snowboard. Now I am not saying that there should not be a limit to the risk involved. There are some activities where involvement is sheer stupidity, but my dad let us pursue many of our natural yearnings as boys.

Fun with Friends

Some of my fondest memories with my friends did not happen at a bowling alley, movie theatre, or stadium. No, some of the best times that Greg, Matt, Adam, Cameron, Ethan, and I had were at the Rainer household. Most teenagers would shun the idea of spending time at home with their friends primarily because of their parents. Let's face it: most teenagers do not consider their parents to be "cool." And I didn't either. However, I did not mind my friends and myself hanging out at our house. In fact, our house became somewhat of the meeting place for the group of guys with which I hung out. Much of this was due to the way my dad handled my friends whenever they came around.

While many of my friends' parents were welcoming and pleasant to be around, my dad was especially so. No matter when they came over, he was glad, even excited to see them. He wanted to talk to them, see how life was going, and ask who they were now dating. He sat with them as long as they wanted to sit with him, no more. And because of this, they grew to like him. They knew that they were accepted and wanted in our house. And when we wanted to be left alone, Dad let us. He did not try to be anybody that he wasn't. He did not try to be "cool" (it wouldn't have worked anyway) to get my friends to like him. He was himself, and that was enough. Because of him, we made many memories.

Undivided Fun

I won't dwell too much on this topic since the idea has been presented a couple of times. Of course, I couldn't dominate all the time with Dad; he had to balance it with his and my brothers' relationships. My father did this very well. He was able to spend time with each of us, having fun the way we liked to have fun, as well as spending time as a group.

Bottom line: My dad and I had fun together and as a group. He encouraged my brothers and me to enjoy life both by ourselves and with friends. He was able to be serious when the time called for it and able to have fun as well. This resulted in many good times had and stories to tell.

Let me be clear. Dad did set limits on the fun we could have. My younger brother, Jess, had some friends come spend the night at our home while Dad was on a trip. My mom awoke at 2:00 a.m. to discover that some of Jess's friends wanted to have fun by getting on our roof to admire the nighttime view.

My poor mom screamed at the boys to get down and immediately called my dad to tell him what was going on. Dad does not like to be awakened—especially at two in the morning to be told that some of Jess's buddies are on the roof.

Enough of that fun. My dad got those boys on the phone, and you should have heard what he said to them. I am tempted to write his words at this point, but then the chapter wouldn't be fun anymore.

I yield to my father's story instead.

— A Father's Perspective —

I think Art is baiting me a bit to tell the story of the boys on the roof. He knows that I blew my temper on that one, and he is just waiting to see if I confess. OK, I confess, but since this is a chapter about fun, I won't spoil the party with details of my moment of outburst.

It is the nature of our family to kid each other, to goad one another with humor, and just to have a good time. I am convinced that one of the successes of parenting in general, and fatherhood in particular, is found in families that laugh frequently and enjoy life with all of its laughs and pleasures.

The world of medical science keeps telling us of new research that demonstrates a positive relationship between laughter and good health. If laughter is a prescription for a healthy life, then you can expect the Rainer family to have a long life span.

Count It All Joy: From One Family to Another

It is my prayer that I have given each of my sons the gift of joy and laughter for their own new homes. Both of my parents taught me that the Christian life should be one of joy and laughter, but my mom particularly had a contagious humor. I think Art in many ways took after his "Nana." I remember seeing my then fifteen-year-old son crying tears of deep grief at his grandmother's funeral. He knew what a precious gift she had been to him and all of the Rainer family.

The first book of the Bible I studied in any depth as a child was Philippians. The apostle Paul, in the midst of his own personal persecution and imprisonment, told the church at Philippi to "Rejoice in the Lord always. I will say it again: Rejoice!" (Phil. 4:4). While I cannot begin to emulate the great apostle, I have learned to rejoice in life. And it seems, at least to hear Art's story, that I have given him and his family the gift of rejoicing.

From my mother to me. From me to Art. I can't wait until the grandchildren start playing jokes on me.

Count it all joy.

Success Stories of Joy

I hope by this point of the book that you understand completely that I have no bragging rights to being a dad. My wife, Nellie Jo, deserves all the human credit, and our Lord simply bestowed grace on me when He gave me three great sons.

While Art's history of my fatherhood is a bit revisionist, I don't want to leave you with the impression that I was a total flop as a dad either. Frankly, there were many times when I helped our family have a blast at life. One of my great sins is my love of '60s music. I sang to my boys, to their total annoyance at times. But even today, they can sing "Red Rubber Ball" with me. Now, I can't sing worth a lick and I can't carry a tune, but it was part of the joy and laughter in the Rainer home.

Nellie Jo often popped paper bags behind the boys and elicited a scream of "Mom!" from them every time. Sam made goat sounds at the drive-up window of the fast-food restaurant. Art was the master of the one-liners. And Jess sold balloons filled with flour at his school as "stress-reduction bags" at a considerable profit. The exercise started as a joke until he saw the entrepreneurial possibilities.

Now, all of these activities may sound like silliness and immaturity. But the Rainer family found great joy in laughing and jokes. We still do to this day.

I grieve when I go to homes filled with tension. I hurt to see children being so careful around their parents lest they break a meaningless rule or engender anger in their mother or father. Life is just too brief to be so uptight.

Art and Sarah's wedding was a tribute to the God who gave us the gift of marriage. It was God-centered in every aspect of the service. The vows that Art and Sarah read to each other left few dry eyes among those of us present. Does that means that this celebration was just not the right place and the right time for laughter? Wrong!

At the reception, the wedding party was introduced with great fanfare to the University of Kentucky fight song. And to add to the joy and laughter, Art enticed the University of Kentucky Wildcat mascot to lead the wedding party into the reception area. Laughter was abundant at the reception as Art and Sarah did the C-A-T-S yell.

I was so proud of my son. The gift of joy and laughter goes on.

But I have not always been so joyous . . .

CONFESSIONS OF A BAH-HUMBUG FATHER

I loved watching my boys participate in sports. One of their youngest ventures was T-Ball. For the uninitiated, T-Ball is baseball without a pitcher. The baseball is placed on a T for the young boy or girl to hit.

Now the beauty of T-Ball is that you can't strike out. If you happen to miss the ball when you swing, your coach will help you position your bat, and you get to try again. In fact, you keep on trying until you finally hit the ball. My boys called second and third swings "do-overs."

I wish I had some do-overs as a father. I tend to be a workaholic. And when I put in long and unreasonable hours, I get grouchy. The laughing and joyous father becomes a bear.

Though I have had many spells of the bah-humbug attitude, it seemed to be especially pervasive when my boys were young. I was a seminary student and pastor of a rural church. I also worked at a bank since the church only provided me fifty dollars per week in income. My schedule was horrendous. Fifteen hours of classroom time each week. Thirty plus hours at the bank. Over twenty hours a week of studying. And at least forty hours at the church.

During those three years, I often was anything but a joy. I have some painful memories that I don't particularly like recalling. But the book would be incomplete without those types of stories.

The three preschool boys were still in their pajamas, watching an early-morning cartoon. "Look at Scooby Doo, Daddy!" one of the boys exclaimed in laughter. Those boys were having so much fun. They wanted their daddy to join in on the hilarity.

I was tired and had to leave for an 8:00 a.m. class, but that does not excuse my behavior. I told the boys in an irritable tone that I had to leave and they needed to hug me good-bye, part of our everyday routine.

The boys were into their cartoons and were oblivious to my demands. In a moment of anger, I left the little campus apartment without my daily hugs. I got into the old Ford, made the usual U-turn that brought me right in front of the apartment. And there, standing on the little porch, were Sam and Art crying, motioning for me to return and hug them.

I felt like such a lowlife—because I was.

Even as I write this story more than two decades later, my eyes are filling with tears.

I jumped out of the car, grabbed my two sons with each of my arms, took them back into the apartment, and hugged them repeatedly.

I then threw off my coat and sat on the floor and watched Scooby Doo.

I missed my 8:00 a.m. class, and I don't even remember what the class was. But I do remember Scooby Doo. And I do remember my boys yelling with delight that Daddy had returned and joined the party of laughter.

But there just aren't any do-overs as a father.

You can ask for forgiveness. You can make up for a bad moment.

But you can't undo that which has already been done.

There are no do-overs.

Understanding the Perspective of the Gift

If there is a single reason that I was able to bring laughter and fun into the Rainer home, it was because of my perspective of the gift.

Please allow me to explain.

When I treated my sons as shamelessly as I told above, I did not get the perspective of the gift. But many times I did.

The first perspective is the gift of life. This brief time on earth escapes so quickly. God has put us here for but a few moments to enjoy the gift of life and to bring glory to Him. It seems that I have blinked my eyes, and those three preschool sons are now grown married men.

I must grasp fully that life is brief and it is a gift from God. It is to be a gift that we celebrate. When I have that perspective, I am a father and husband of joy and laughter. I am delighted with life and enjoy it to the fullest.

There is a second perspective to the gift. From the time I was a child, I wanted children. God has allowed me to see my boys as incredible gifts from Him. That's why I show such delight in them. That's why I have so much laughter when I am around them. I know that God does not bless everyone with the gift of children, and I am no more deserving than the childless couple. That is why they are gifts. Grace-filled gifts.

I wish every father could read these next few lines. Men, our children are more important than our work. They are more important than our days on the golf course or hours in front of the television. The legacy we leave is not how much money we earned or what level of status we received. The legacy we leave is our children. Take delight in them. Have joy in them. Laugh with them.

February 6, 2006. An important day for me, but not the most important day for me.

The day was my inauguration to be the ninth president of LifeWay Christian Resources. I had never expected such an honor would come my way, and I certainly did not seek it.

LifeWay was filled with dignitaries, friends, family, and employees who had come for this day. Van Ness Auditorium filled quickly, and many people moved to overflow rooms.

It was a great day, but the shining stars of that day were not me, but my three sons. I had determined at the onset of the planning of the inauguration that the event would not be complete unless Sam, Art, and Jess spoke. I don't think that a president has ever done that, but I knew it was right for me. Those boys are such gifts.

After some preliminary fanfare, my family was introduced. Nellie Jo received a prolonged standing ovation. (Everybody always likes her more than me.) And then came the introductions of the three boys. They were to speak in reverse birth order, so Jess went first, followed by Art and Sam.

Those boys had the audience rolling in laughter. Each of them told stories and had one-liners that reflected the laughter and joy and fun in which they had been raised. And they spoke words of tribute to me that I refuse to write here. Suffice to say, they left me in tears. I could hardly speak when they were done.

Let there be no doubt that I am proud to be the president of LifeWay Christian Resources. It is an unspeakable joy and honor. But you certainly know where my greatest joy and pride came that day. I cried as the audience stood and applauded

Nellie Jo. I wept as each boy spoke. I am so proud of my family. I love them so very much. They are gifts, incredible gifts.

I think my boys know that. Art certainly has articulated that in this book. We are a family of joy. We are a family of laughter and fun. And we are a family that loves each other with intensity.

I thank God that He has given me that perspective with my sons. And I wish I had kept that perspective every day while the boys were still at home.

Thanks for the laughter, Art.

Thanks for the fun.

Thanks for the love.

What a gift.

What an incredible gift.

Chapter 7

───~~~~~~───

Love: Saying It and Showing It

Did you ever worry while growing up that your parents would eventually find out who you *really* were, what you *really* did when they weren't around, that the person you portrayed was just a façade? Occasionally I run into parents who seem to think that their child is better, more innocent, than he or she actually is. This is especially so as the child becomes a teenager or young adult. A hazy cloud of idealism hangs over reality and prevents these parents from seeing their children clearly. They think that their child is the exception—not like the other kids, not like his or her friends. Their kids are the good kids. Their kids are different.

Children pick up quickly on their parents' idealistic view and enjoy being treated like the image they portray. This can drive the kids to hide any wrong that has been done, any mistakes that have been made. What child would want to move from underneath the shade of their parents praise and approval?

This was especially true for me, the son of a pastor. I felt as if there were certain expectations of me, and I had little room for mistakes. When I went to college, I felt that I was finally free to do as I pleased—as long as my parents did not find out what I did. I lived much of my college life this way, partying while at school and attending church while at home. I thought that my parents would never know the difference. They didn't. In their eyes, I was still the greatest son in the world (sorry, Jess and Sam). I was two different people in two different cities.

I had gotten pretty far off the "straight and narrow" by the end of my sophomore year in college. I had lived the typical fraternity lifestyle and all that it entails. My relationship with God was not strong. I was becoming more and more wayward. However, in the thick of it all I had applied with a Christian organization for a mission/spiritual-growth trip to San Diego for the summer, and I got accepted. Admittedly, there were parts on the application that I lied about—not a proud moment for me.

While out in San Diego, I was placed with a mentor who would be there to keep me spiritually accountable throughout the summer. His name was Jay. One day Jay and I were in a pretty deep conversation while walking on the beach. He started asking questions about my personal life. For some reason, I didn't feel like lying to him, and I decided to let it pour out. I told him the truth about who I had become. I told him of all that had happened in the first two years of my college life and that I was tired of it, weary of the lifestyle. I did not want a repeat performance when I returned for the fall semester.

After discussing my spiritual fallout, Jay recommended that I make a drastic move to ensure that I remain on course. He told me to think of the person whom I admired most in my life.

I said, "My dad."

Jay told me that I needed to call my father and tell him all that I had just told him. He claimed that this would help me declare a turning point in my life. It would shine a light on everything that I had hidden so well in darkness. It would help me cross a line and never turn back.

"It's your decision. Pray about it," he said.

Needless to say, I was extremely hesitant about this idea. Can you imagine calling up your father or mother and telling them all of the wrong that you have done? Who would do that? I felt that there were some things that were better left unsaid. It seemed borderline crazy to me. In fact, I had no plans of doing this at first. I could handle this on my own. My parents did not need to be involved.

The next couple of days were rough. God continued to put what Jay had said on my heart. It was heavy, and I could not get it off my mind. I knew what God wanted me to do. I didn't want to, but I had to. When I gave in, I cried. I don't cry very often, and honestly, I could not pinpoint the reason why I cried. Maybe it was fear of the phone call that I knew was about to take place, or maybe I was just overwhelmed with the whole experience of God's overpowering yank on my life. Whatever the reason, it was a real cry because something real had taken place.

I grabbed my cell phone and sat on the nearest curb, heart pounding.

My dad answered the phone in the way he always does, "What's up, buddy?"

"Not much. Look, Dad, I am just going to get to the point."

I proceeded to tell all that I had done while being away at school. It was very humbling, and all during my confession, I could not even imagine what my father's thoughts would be of me from that point on. Finally, I finished and waited for a response from my dad.

"Well, son, as you know I definitely don't condone anything that you did, but, as always, I love you, and that will never change."

That was it. That's all he said.

The word *love* is very confusing in our English vocabulary. It is a feeling. It is something that you do. I remember telling my first-grade crush, Annie, that I loved her, but she didn't love me back. Love takes on so many different shapes and forms. Some view love with such deep meaning that they use it only when referring to certain people, such as their wife and kids. Some are willing to tell anyone with whom they are acquainted that they love them. Some say that unless you are willing to die for someone, you do not truly love that person. Others would think that this notion is crazy and tell you to "love all."

If I told you, the reader, right now that I loved you, how would *you* take it? You might think that I was insane because I do not even know you. Or you could think that this is the way that the world ought to be, loving anyone, even the unknown.

Some of you may turn to a more theological view of love and look at all the different types of love in the Greek language and what they mean. One type of love is a physical attraction. Another is a friendship. And yet another is a powerful, completely unconditional love.

I do know that my father's love for me was pretty amazing. Much like the love of God, I sometimes get frustrated when I sit down and try to figure it out. It's baffling. I can't really put a definition to it, so I will do my best to somehow convey the love I receive even beyond my childhood. I hope I do it justice.

UNCONDITIONAL LOVE

"Now remember boys, Daddy loves you, and Jesus does too! Good night!"

After our prayers, this was the nightly phrase that my father left with my brothers and me before exiting our room at bedtime.

A love that is unconditional is incredible, if not unbelievable. It continues when embarrassed, ridiculed, mocked, lied to, rebelled against, or anything else, good or bad. The truth is that unconditional love is just that, unconditional. No matter what happens, that love is always there. Though tested and strained, it continues to endure, and it stretches as far as the eye can see and as deep as the human mind can fathom. There is a mysterious power to it that can be felt but not explained.

My dad's love was, and still is, unconditional. Knowing that was vital to me as a child. There will not be many people in life that we can say love us without hesitation, but we all need someone who will do this for us—someone we can turn to when things get rough, knowing we will not be judged. For a child, that love needs to come from his or her parents.

I was blessed. I knew that no matter what I did, my dad would love me. Though he might get angry at the things that I did or the torment I caused (and there were several opportunities to test this theory), his love would remain. The result of this type of love was an inner confidence. I knew that I had someone who loved me regardless of what I did. I did not have to prove myself to him, as some children do, to get his love. I was able to be myself because that was enough. That was all it took. I was able to pursue my own desires and passions. I did not have to prove myself to get Dad's love. It was unconditional.

Undivided Love

As I have mentioned a couple of times now, my parents did their best to make sure that we were treated equally. This equal treatment meant that they never wanted to show favoritism of one child over another.

I can imagine that many parents with more than one child struggle with the issue of favoritism. How terrible it must be for a kid to feel that he is loved less than his or her siblings. I have friends who insist that they were the least loved in their family. It is sad and possibly harmful.

Growing up, there were always moments when my brothers and I blindly thought that one child was being loved more than the others. For example, if I punched Jess, he would go and cry to my dad. Amazingly, I would get punished and nothing would happen to Jess. Did Jess do anything? Not really. But clearly, my dad loved Jess more than me! And such are the thoughts of a young child. But those moments were fleeting. It is clear that my dad truly loved us all equally.

When we three boys were young, my father was concerned that one of us might feel that we were being loved less than the others, so he would bluntly ask, "Do you feel like I love Sam or Jess more than you?" And I would give him an honest answer, most of the time with a "no." However, I guarantee that if

I told him that I truly felt that way, he would go out of his way to make sure that I knew that he loved me just as much as my brothers.

Dad concerned himself so much with loving us equally that I now have no question about his love for my brothers and me. Whether his efforts were natural, or intentional and deliberate, he made certain that his love was distributed equally.

It's amazing, even today, when I hear my peers talk about how they were not the favored one among their siblings. Though they may seem to be only joking, I can still hear the hurt in their voices and see the hurt in their eyes. When a child honestly feels that they have been placed at a lower importance than their sibling, dealing with it can become incredibly difficult and could carry over far into the adult years. Some may even feel an inadequacy or have a bitterness that they take to their grave. Hopefully this is the minority. Favoritism is painful, and the wounds can run deep.

SAYING IT WITH WORDS

If you have not caught on yet, my dad was very verbal about his love to my brothers and me. He unashamedly told us, my mom, his friends, church congregation, relatives, strangers, coworkers, or anyone else with whom he came into contact. If family was brought up in a conversation, he would tell of his love for his sons without hesitation. He literally *loved* telling of his love for us.

And though he would tell so many people, the most important people to hear those three words were named Sam, Art, and Jess. It is vitally important for a father to verbally tell his children that he loves them. The feeling that a child receives from the confirmation of his father's love is incredible. Even in my teenage years, when I didn't think it was "cool" for my dad to tell me that he loved me in front of my peers, I am glad that at least *he* was not embarrassed. Dad would never let me question his love for me. Saying "I love you" is so simple, and yet it can have such a tremendous impact on a child.

SHOWING IT

A hug. That is how my dad physically showed me that he loved me. Sometimes a bear hug and sometimes a side hug, but always a hug. Even now, when I am older, he still hugs me and has never resorted to a handshake. A handshake conveys respect, not love; there is a difference. We greet with a hug and say our good-byes with a hug.

I think that when you truly love someone, there is a desire to have physical contact from the other person. There is an intimacy involved in acts such as hugging that says you are more than just an acquaintance; you are a loved one.

I am so glad that my dad showed me the way to love physically. Especially for us guys, it is sometimes out of our comfort zone to have physical contact with others outside of a handshake. There is a time and place for everything, but between those who truly love one another, physical contact is a clear way to show the feelings of your heart.

LOVE: A SON'S CONCLUDING NOTE

The most important aspect of my dad's love for me lies in his love for me as a brother in Christ. From this love stems all of the other love of which I have just written. It is from this outflow that I feel he is able to show his heart to us the way that he has and still does. I do not know if parents can truly love their children the way they ought without loving them as a Christian brother or sister first. It is a supernatural love that goes well beyond what we, as humans, can produce on our own. It is a gift from God.

My father loved me with the love of the Father. It is little wonder that I grew up with such a feeling of total security. I knew that I was loved.

— A Father's Perspective —

I have a surprise for Art. I never thought that he was perfect. Indeed, I never thought that his brothers were perfect. Now, I did not know the details of their imperfections and, to some extent, I did not want to know all the details. But I knew of some things about my boys that they did not realize I knew.

And I am not surprised that any of my sons had their moments of rebellion and bad behavior in high school and college. So when Art had that tough telephone conversation with me from San Diego, I was neither shocked nor unprepared.

Yes, there was some disappointment as I listened. But never, never, never did I love my son any less at the conclusion of that conversation. Please allow me to share some reasons why I survived well Art's confessions to me.

First, I accept as a theological reality the depravity of humanity. I believe without hesitation that "all have sinned and fall short of the glory of God" (Rom. 3:23). And, if I had been totally honest with Art during that conversation, I would have let him know that his old man committed similar acts of rebellion in college. In fact, I would be willing to wager that Art was much better than I, even at his worst moments.

Second, my wife and I pray fervently and regularly for our boys. We ask the Father who is with them at all times to protect them in their moments of rebellion. And we ask God to direct them towards paths of righteousness. Simply stated, we have entrusted our sons to a Father who loves them even more than we do.

Third, I accept the moments of disappointment with my boys because the moments of joy far outweigh the less joyous moments. They have given me so much happiness that I am willing to accept those times when I am a bit disappointed.

One great experience I had recently took place when I was being introduced before I spoke to a large crowd. The person introducing me said, "And one thing that we have all come to love about Thom Rainer is how much he loves his family. I imagine that before Dr. Rainer finishes speaking tonight, you will hear something about his sons."

He was right.

In fact, since I have been on the speaking circuit for some fifteen years, people often come up to me and ask me about my sons. Through my writings and speeches, they have come to love the Rainer family, and they want updates on the boys and Nellie Jo.

I just love those boys.

THE UNCONDITIONAL LOVE OF A FATHER

The apostle Paul gives a vivid description of *agape* love in 1 Corinthians 13. The context is a church that is divided on many issues, and Paul sees the need to get to the heart of the issue: lack of love for one another.

He then gives a powerful description of unconditional love: "Love is patient; love is kind. Loves does not envy; is not boastful; is not conceited; does not act improperly; is not selfish; is not provoked; does not keep a record of wrongs; finds no joy in unrighteousness, but rejoices in truth; bears all things, believes all things, hopes all things, endures all things" (1 Cor. 13:4–7).

I have no man-made explanation for the unconditional love I have for my sons. It can only be explained by the love that has been given to me by my Father.

May I speak bluntly to you fathers who are reading this book? I do not believe that you can grasp unconditional love until you first experience it. And the only way to experience it is by accepting the love of the Father in heaven.

When I was a teenager, my high school coach shared with me about this unconditional love. Coach Joe explained to me how we are all separated from God by our sin, and that all have sinned. The bad news is that everyone is separated from God by sin and will not go to heaven.

The good news is that Jesus Christ took the punishment for our sins. He literally became our substitute by dying on the cross. Through His shed blood and death, He paid the penalty, and we can have forgiveness of our sins.

I grasped that reality as a teenager and prayed a simple prayer: "Lord, I know I am a sinner, but I also know that Jesus died for my sins. Please forgive my sins. I accept you as my Lord and Savior."

I accepted by faith what Jesus did for me on the cross. It was a gift, an act of grace. I did nothing to deserve my salvation. I did nothing to earn it. I received unconditional love.

Fathers, the first step to giving unconditional love is to receive unconditional love. If you have never received the gift of salvation through Jesus Christ, I invite you right now to pause from the reading of this book. I invite you to speak to God, to confess your sins, to receive the unmerited gift of salvation through Jesus Christ. I invite you to know fully unconditional love.

I can love my sons unconditionally because I have experienced *agape* love. The apostle Paul calls it "the greatest of these" (1 Cor. 13:13).

No Favorites in Parenting

I can say without reservation or hesitation that I do not love one son more than another. I can also say without hesitation or reservation that I sometimes seem to show favoritism. If the two statements sound contradictory, please let me explain by illustration.

You have read in this book how Art got to live his dream of becoming a football player. And his younger brother, Jess, was able to benefit from Art's persistence in getting his school to start a football team. In fact, Jess's senior football team finished fifth in the state after the football program had been in existence only five years. And the football stadium that the school built was one of the best in the state.

In case you didn't know it, I love football.

I was in the stands screaming at every game.

I was one of the most obnoxious parents in the stadium.

And I loved every minute of it.

Art and Jess knew their dad was there for them. They knew that I was passionate about their playing football. They knew that

I would literally get sick to my stomach from excitement before each game.

But Sam didn't play football.

Let me be clear. Sam couldn't play football because the team was not formed until the year after he graduated from high school. And he had such great football skills. I am convinced that he would have been an outstanding wide receiver.

But Sam didn't play football.

Now, don't get me wrong. I loved watching Sam play basketball. His team went to the "sweet 16" for one of his four high school years. And I loved watching him run track. I was so proud when he qualified for the state track meet. I was there in total enthusiasm.

But I just couldn't get into his cross country meets. There was something about watching a crowd of people run away from you, and then you don't see anything for some time. Finally some runners come struggling to the finish line. Others soon follow. Some get sick and never finish. And I think some get abducted by aliens because they are nowhere to be found.

I confess that I did not give Sam's cross country meets the priority that I should have. I should not have let my lack of enthusiasm for the sport be so evident.

I know Sam had to compare my enthusiasm for football to my lackluster support of his cross country meets.

I did show favoritism. I confess. But I showed favoritism toward a sport, not a son.

And I do not love one son more than the others.

Thank God for their mother, my wife. She was there for them. It didn't matter what they were involved in, she was there for them. Nellie Jo doesn't know that a balk belongs to baseball, that a brick is something that happens in basketball, and that a bomb is thrown in football. She may not know the difference between a balk, a brick, and a bomb, but she is much better than I am.

I don't have favorites among my sons. But she made certain her actions never hinted of favoritism.

I guess Art did not see that perspective of my favoritism.

And if I had to do it over again, I would be at every cross country meet screaming for the kids who have run away so far that you can't see them. And I would be searching for those poor souls before they got abducted by aliens.

I would not have favorites . . . and I would make certain my actions supported my heart.

WORDS SPOKEN ARE WORDS REMEMBERED

You read earlier that my father was a quiet and reticent man. I knew that he loved me, but I rarely heard him speak verbally of his affection for me. And here I am, a man more than a half-century old, and I am still talking about it.

One of the most vivid memories of my dad was in my young adult years, only two years before his death. As I noted earlier, I came from a long line of bankers, but I was about to break the tradition.

God had called me to full-time vocational ministry.

Thoughts of worry raced through my mind. What will Dad think? Will he get mad? Will he be so disappointed that he will be left speechless?

The day approached for my meeting with Dad and Mom. With a trembling voice, I told my father of my call and my response. There was a pause of a few seconds that seemed like a few hours. Then Dad spoke, softly but firmly: "I am so proud of you son."

I cried.

I cried because I was relieved. But I also cried because Dad told me he was proud of me. He *told* me. Verbally. I knew Dad loved me. And I knew he was proud of me. But I was desperate to hear it, and I heard it so rarely.

You have heard throughout this book my countless mistakes and dumb decisions as a father. I make no claims to perfection. Far from it. But I have never hesitated in telling my boys that I love them, that I am proud of them, and that I find no greater joy than being with them. I *tell* them.

As long as I am alive and have a voice to speak, I will tell them how I feel. Every child needs to hear words of affirmation from his or her parents. And they need a regular diet of it.

THE TOUCH

All my friends make fun of me. They know that I am not a touchy-feely person. I avoid hugs from others. In fact, I get uptight when my space is invaded.

Rich is a good friend whom I have known for more than a decade. He lives in Atlanta, so we see each other infrequently. But when he does see me, he comes running toward me to give me a bear hug. I first try to run from him, but if I am unsuccessful, I cringe and become tense the moment he touches me. My friends love to watch the predictable scene.

But I have always hugged my boys. My wife, Nellie Jo, would hand me the boys continuously when they were babies. I once thought that she did so to take a break. But now I see that she had a greater purpose. She wanted me to bond physically with my sons at the earliest possible age.

I hugged those boys from birth to present. I kissed them on the cheeks when they were young boys. I would wrestle with them on the floor and tickle them crazy. And I would play wayuphigh with them.

Wayuphigh? Huh?

Wayuphigh became one of the favorite activities of my young sons. They would tell me, "Daddy, take me way up high!" I would then lie on my back, put a son on the top of my raised legs and feet, and lift him "way up high" in the air.

And you know, I don't think that they were particularly impressed with the modest heights my stocky legs lifted them. They just loved the attention and physical contact with their dad.

Have you read the accounts of babies in orphanages overseas who are not regularly touched, hugged, or spoken to? Have you read how they are motionless and lifeless even though they have no physical problems? Those tragic stories are real because those children have been deprived of human touch and words.

The touch.

I will hug my boys until the day I die.

Art and Sarah's wedding was a great event. It was filled with reverence, laughter, and joy. God was truly honored.

After a rather long reception, my newly married son was ready to leave. Now I know I'm not supposed to hinder newlyweds on their wedding night. But I had to see Art for just a minute.

The room was somewhat dark, so I don't think he saw the tears in my eyes. Tears of joy. "I am so proud of you, buddy," I said with a voice that struggled with emotions. And I hugged him. And I told him I loved him.

I started doing that when he was a baby.

I have no plans to stop now.

Chapter 8

~~~~~~~~

That Time Thing

That day with my dad was certainly memorable, but the story he was told about it several years later made it even more memorable.

Dad was at one of his several speaking engagements at a church conference center when a man approached him during a brief break between speaking sessions.

"Thom, you probably don't know me, but I sure know you," said the man.

My father, taken a little off guard replied, "Oh really? And how's that?"

"A conference that you did a little while back in a suburb of Seattle, Washington, was the most memorable meetings that I have ever been to."

A little flattered, my dad responded, "Well, thank you. I greatly appreciate your telling me that."

Realizing that my dad had just taken his comments as a compliment, the man stepped back and appeared very serious.

"I said it was the most *memorable,* not the best conference that I have been to. There is a difference."

Thrown off guard again, my father said, "I'm sorry. I think that you are going to have to explain yourself a little better. I am not quite sure what you are talking about."

Since my dad speaks all around the nation, remembering one specific conference's details can become a little difficult.

"Well, let me tell you what happened," the man eagerly volunteered. "You had brought one of your sons with you. He seemed to be a nice kid. We had just finished up one of the sessions, and you went into the hallway to talk to your son during the break as you had the past couple of times. He had stayed out there while the sessions were going on so that he wouldn't get bored with us."

Dad gave a quick, "Uh huh."

"However, this time when you went out into the hall, your son was gone. In a moment of panic, you checked the bathrooms, other classrooms, and the rest of the building inside and out. Your kid was nowhere to be found. Finally, you announced to everyone at the conference that your son was missing and that we needed to all go out and search for him before the next session started.

"Well, we did just that. We searched throughout the building and the surrounding area and still could not find your boy. By this time, you were really getting stressed out, and so were we because the next session should have already started by now. We didn't want to go into overtime with this thing.

"Finally, we heard someone yell from down the street, 'I've found him! Here he is!' And lo and behold here comes your son, strolling up the street, having no idea that his father and more than two hundred people had been searching for him.

"You asked him where he had been, and he told you that he had walked to the small downtown area just beyond sight from the conference center. You didn't seem too mad, just relieved. Your wife would've probably killed you, wouldn't she?"

"Well," was all my dad could get out before the man started talking again.

"Since your kid was found, we all filed back into the building to finish up the meeting. That was the only time I have ever done something like that at a conference: look for the speaker's missing child. I'm glad we found him, but it sure did take up a lot of time. That is why I said that the conference was memorable. I will never forget it, no matter how many more meetings I attend."

Having explained himself, he walked off. Dad could only stand there with his mouth still partly opened from trying to get in a word, a little confused and a little shocked at what had just transpired.

I have gone on several trips with my dad, and each hold their own memories. My dad came up with the idea of taking his sons along with him on his business trips in order to spend more time with us. He hated that he had to spend time away from his family and regretted missing a single moment at home. Taking one of his boys along allowed him to spend quality time with at least one of us while he had to be away.

The result of this idea was that he spent a tremendous amount of time with his sons. From Seattle, Washington, to Charlotte, North Carolina, we would travel to speaking engagements, and when we would go on these trips with him, we would spend almost every single moment, from the departure to the return at the airport, together. We spent many moments together that I would never take back.

It is understandable that not every father can take their children on their business trips. My dad was blessed because he had millions of frequent flier miles that allowed us to fly free. However, it was not the trip that made these moments important. It was that my father had found a way to spend time with his children. My father's jobs are probably more time consuming than most, but he did not want that fact to stop him from being with us. He understood the importance of time spent with his children, and he tried to figure out ways to make this vital piece of the relationship happen.

QUANTITY TIME

"Quality, not quantity" is how the saying goes. I get a little irked when I hear this phrase used regarding relationships. Therefore I want to discuss the quantity of time my father spent with my brothers and me first. Now, I know that both the quantity and quality of time are important, but frankly, I wanted my dad to spend *lots* of time with me because from that quantity of time flowed time of quality.

Especially when I was younger, when I knew nothing about the concept of "quality time," the amount of time spent with my father was far more important than what we did with that time. I wanted him to be there to sit and watch a football game, play catch, or visit my grandparents. I wanted to hang out at his office at church, sit in his lap, and play with our dogs, Mike and Joey, with him.

We didn't even have to be doing anything that would be constituted as "quality time," I just wanted him to be there with me. After seeing my older brother graduate from the University of South Carolina, Dad and I had to make the long car trip from Columbia, South Carolina, to Louisville, Kentucky. Not many words were said on this trip. We were both pretty exhausted. If you had ridden along with us, you probably would have gone through several bouts of boredom because the excitement of the journey was minimal. Yet, it is one of my favorite memories. We were together, and that was enough. Quantity somehow became quality.

I believe that quality time can be planned, and fathers can set aside certain periods to spend with their children. But so many of my valued memories came from times when no plans were made. Some of those moments transpired when we were simply together with no agenda. For the most part, it is natural for us to share our deepest thoughts and feelings with those with whom we are closest and spend the most amount of time. The moments when I opened up most to my dad were when we had spent extended periods of time together. Maybe it is just coincidence. Maybe not.

Church camps are a great example of quantity leading to quality time. From breakfast to lights out at night, you spend every waking moment with a bunch of kids—some you have known for a long time and some you just met. It's weird that towards the end of the week, almost everyone starts opening up, sharing their feelings, their crushes with the girls in the next cabins, their struggles with life. Tears are shed, and hugs are given without hesitation. There is a certain bond just because you have shared a week with them, and you feel that you can tell them anything. You become each other's confidants. It happens every single time. You can count on it.

A very similar response happened when I spent a large amount of time with my father on the trips that I mentioned earlier. For that moment, he became the one with whom I shared anything. I had just spent an extensive amount of time with him, and I felt closer, more willing to become vulnerable. I would open up and tell my dad things that I wouldn't have mentioned otherwise. Suddenly, he became my best friend; he became my confidant. Coincidence? Maybe. Probably not.

QUALITY TIME

As I said before, I do believe that quality time is important, and it seems to directly stem from the amount of time spent with each other. Some see quality time as moments purposefully spent with another to create a deeper and more lasting bond. Blessed are the parents who realize: "This time spent will be important to me and my children for the present and the future." Many great parents are intentional about creating these valued moments, and my father was as well.

In the first chapter, I discussed how my father purposefully made memories. He planned moments such as going to McDonald's on Saturday mornings to spend time with his children and create moments that my brothers and I would remember for the rest of our lives.

His intentional efforts to create quality time were very important to me as a child. My father purposefully set aside time to spend with me, and it sent the message that I was important and loved. As a child, I was a priority in my dad's life. That was clear to me. He wanted to be with me as much as I wanted to be with him.

SEPARATING WORK AND FAMILY

"Do you feel like I am working too much?"

"Do you feel like I don't spend enough time at home?"

"Do I go on too many business trips?"

"Will you be upset if I go on this trip and miss your game?"

"Do you want me to come home?"

These are just a few of the questions that my dad would ask my brothers and me as he began to travel more during my high school years. He was constantly interrogating us so he could see how we were truly feeling, sometimes to the point of annoying us. My dad cared deeply about the time he spent with his family, and he did not want work to come between him and his relationship with the family.

Up until my high school years, Dad's travels were limited. He made sure that he could stay home as much as possible so that he would not miss any portion of his children's lives. My father wanted to be there for the times when we needed him as well as the times when we did not need him. He was constantly around, and that is the way he wanted it. My brothers and I took priority over any meeting or function, and except for an occasional church service, he would cancel any engagements without hesitation if he felt that he needed to spend more time with us. Because of this, I never questioned his commitment to me, his son.

Even when my dad's travels began to increase, he made sure that he could be there for us. For our sporting events, he would schedule his speaking engagements around our games (which is a daunting task with three athletic sons). Only rarely would he miss one of our games.

When he felt that his schedule was becoming too busy and he was away from home too much, he would ask us our feelings on the issue. He did not presuppose that we were fine with everything. In fact, he assumed the worst, that we needed him back home for longer periods of time. Only rarely would one of us admit that we wished he would stay home from a trip, and when that happened, without hesitation he dropped whatever engagement was scheduled. Most of the time, my dad exaggerated the amount of time spent away from home. He was so concerned with not making the same mistake his father made that it almost became an obsession for him. I can only hope that all dads obsess the same way my father did.

TIME WITH HIS WIFE

In a chapter that is dedicated to the time my father spent with me, I feel it necessary to point out that my mom was not left out either. It is important for a child to see that his mother holds a special place in the heart of his or her father. This dedicated time becomes more problematic as children suddenly, and sometimes unexpectedly, invade the home. Precious time that was shared between parents suddenly lessens as they begin to focus on their children.

I remember my parents actively participating in, or should I say, "taking advantage of," our church's "Parents' Night Out." These events were held so that parents could drop their kids off at the church so they could go spend time together, alone as a couple. Though I did not fully understand at that time why they needed to spend time alone, away from us kids, I now look back on those times and smile. My dad loved my mom and wanted to spend time with her just as much, if not more, than he wanted to spend time with us. He treasured my mom then as much as he does now. I cannot fathom the difference this probably made in our household. Just like his children, my mom knew that she was a priority in her husband's life.

This is so important for me to look back and see. As I approached my wedding day, I began to see even more the importance of showing my wife that she is special, set apart from everything else in my life. Just like children, she needs to be shown that she is loved and a priority. It is a commitment that cannot be compromised.

I would not take back any of the time spent with my dad, and as I grow older, I become more aware of the importance of spending priceless moments with my father. We are only given a brief lifetime to make memories with one another, and as this opportunity becomes more limited, I become more anxious than ever to spend time with my father. One day, one of us will pass away to our eternity, and that time spent will become invaluable. No dollar amount will be able to retrieve any time that has been lost between us. Moments of time will then only be found in our memories.

I now have more fun with my dad than I ever did as a child, and this issue is key: time spent with your children does not stop after they leave the household. Continue to pursue valued moments with your child as if they were still in their youth.

Time is brief. Time is precious. Time is a gift from God. Do not squander it.

This I promise you: After one of you dies, neither will look back to regret a single moment that you spent together.

— A Father's Perspective —

Ugh.

I dreaded this chapter. Art made all the decisions about chapter content. It was to be his book, with my responses. I knew that the time issue would arise. And I knew that honesty would compel me to respond in ways that I do not find pleasant.

If I could end this chapter with only Art's perspective, I would seem to be one super dad. But I am not. I struggle significantly in this area. Let me share, with reluctance and humility, the areas of my struggle.

CONFESSIONS OF A WORKAHOLIC

I don't know why I am so driven. My dad was a successful businessman in our small town, but he sure wasn't a workaholic. He never missed opportunities to fish, hunt, and nap. And my mother was a stay-at-home mom most of my childhood. She always found time for me and her friends.

There is definitely a positive side to my disposition. I am able to accomplish much. I am a dreamer and a visionary. But now I am bragging. I guess I'm avoiding addressing the issue of this chapter.

I am a workaholic.

And that workaholism caused me to neglect my sons more often than I am comfortable discussing.

I find comfort in Art's perspective. He said that I exaggerated my time away from the boys. But I think he is seeing me through rose-colored glasses.

Now he is right in some respects. I did schedule my speaking engagements around their activities. And I did, for the most part, limit my time away to no more than two consecutive nights. But I still was gone too much. I just don't agree with Art's assessment. I did not do well in this area.

I have attempted to psychoanalyze my workaholic tendencies. Some of my time spent writing books and speaking in cities across the world was a true desire on my part to do ministry. I love watching Christians get excited about sharing their faith. And I am passionate about seeing churches become more evangelistic. If my books and speeches contribute to that reality, then I am one happy camper.

And, I must admit that some of my motivation was financial. For a dozen years, I taught and served as a dean of a seminary. It was almost a necessity for me to supplement my income with the modest wages of academia.

But I would be less than honest if I failed to mention another motivation that contributes to my workaholism. I received great ego fulfillment when I was on the road, especially in the early years of that ministry. Though I am not the best-known speaker and writer in the world, there are people who actually listen to me and read my books.

I wonder how many times I neglected my family because I enjoyed the accolades of others. I wonder how many times Sam, Art, Jess, and Nellie Jo longed for the presence of their father and husband when I was basking in the compliments of other people. I really don't want to guess. It hurts too much to think about it.

Art thought I spent quantity time with him and his brothers. I hope I did. But my perspective is just not as sunny as his. I failed many times.

CONFESSIONS OF A DISTRACTED FATHER

Two confessions in one chapter. No wonder I dreaded this part of the book. You see, I not only was absent physically from my boys too often, I was also absent in spirit at times. I have one story among many that highlights this deficiency too clearly.

The year was 1988. Art was a six-year-old at that point, Sam was eight, and Jess was five. It was late spring, and all the boys were involved in baseball. Between the three of them, I bet we had eight to ten practices and ball games a week.

I was serving as pastor of a church in the area. The congregation had grown significantly, and I had moved from part-time to full-time status. And to add to my schedule, I was finishing a PhD. All of the seminar and class work had been completed, but I had a dissertation to finish with only three months left on my deadline. So I took my work with me to the baseball field and actually worked on my project during a game.

Bad move.

My wife's frustration with me was mild but noticeable. I decided to keep on working since mild frustration was OK with me.

Another bad move.

Then it happened. Art was at bat. "Thomas, Art is batting. You need to pay attention to the game," Nellie Jo spoke softly. "I am," I lied. I was into my writing.

What did Art do? He hit a ball to the fence that drove in two runs. He had a triple, almost an in-the-park home run.

And I missed it.

My wife's frustration with me was not the worst part. That came after the game. "Dad, did you see my triple?" Art asked expectantly. "I drove in the winning runs!"

I could not lie. All I could do was tell him I didn't see it until he made it to third base. The look of disappointment on his face is still with me two decades later.

I have many faults. Prominent among them is my lack of focus on things that really matter because I am too focused on that which does not matter nearly as much.

It is one thing to give our children time. But it's another thing to give them our undivided focus and attention. My driven personality not only moves me to do too much to the detriment of my family, but my attention deficit when I am with them is far too common.

I sat at the computer for more than fifteen minutes remembering all those times that I was away from home, or absent in spirit when I was at home with the boys. Do you know what is so incredibly sad? I can hardly remember why I was absent most of the time. In other words, whatever I was doing that took me away from my family was not so important that I can even remember it today. And yet I remember almost every moment I spent with the boys. And you know which of those times were the most important.

RELUCTANT ACCEPTANCE OF A
FEW THINGS DONE RIGHT

I guess you see two different personalities in me, comparing Art's perspectives to my own. I am convinced that a child desires so much to see the best in his or her parents that they will quickly forgive and forget most of the mess-ups we parents make. The description of love in the previous chapter says it well: "[Love] does not keep a record of wrongs" (1 Cor. 13:5).

But I will reluctantly accept a few of Art's accolades. He is right: if my boys ever told me that I was gone too much, any of them had veto privilege. That means that they had the right to cancel any of my travels for any length of time.

Now I know that my precious sons would never test this promise just to test it. Can you guess where the first cancellation took place? Hawaii. All expenses paid for both Nellie Jo and me. One of our sons simply told me that he had missed me because I had been gone so much. Why couldn't we have missed Montana in the winter?

The second cancellation? The white sands of Cape San Blas, Florida. And there have been several other cancellations. And I need to express my deep gratitude to all the churches and organizations that have allowed me to cancel. They have had to scramble at the last minute for a speaker, and they have accepted my explanations of family needs without complaint.

In fact, I can think of only one place that told me they would not let me cancel. My oldest son was being ordained to the ministry and my wife was in chemotherapy treatment. I canceled anyway, much to their anger.

But that is one angry host out of perhaps a dozen cancellations over ten years. I am forever thankful to these hosts for their gracious spirits.

I will also accept the compliment from Art that I attempted to make every event in which they were involved. And some of those times where I made efforts to be at those events are stories in themselves. Allow me to share one.

I had it all figured out. My speaking engagement in St. Louis would be over at 1:00 p.m. I could catch a flight to Louisville, our home at the time, connecting through Cincinnati, and be on the ground at 5:00 p.m.

Art was one of the senior athletes being recognized at the beginning of the basketball game. With the game starting at 7:00 p.m., I had a two-hour cushion. No sweat—until I got to the St. Louis airport to discover that my flight had been canceled.

Panic. I couldn't miss Art's senior night. Nellie Jo and I were to walk with him out to the center of the basketball court. I had to be there. But all the flight options couldn't get me to Louisville on time.

I made a quick decision. I would get a one-way rental car and drive to Louisville. The only problem was that, if I left immediately, with a time-zone change and a five-hour trip, it was doubtful if I could get to the school in time.

But I had no choice. I had to give it a shot.

Nellie Jo kept in touch with me by cell phone most of the trip, especially as time drew closer to the start of the game. The 7:00 p.m. estimated start time was based on the completion of a junior varsity game that preceded the varsity game.

I prayed much of my trip. "Lord, please let me make it to Art's senior night. Please don't let me let him down."

It was 6:15 p.m. when Nellie Jo called. The JV game was about over. That meant that Art's introduction would take place in 30 minutes. But I was still 60 minutes from the school.

I was devastated.

I begin to pray for a miracle. Shortly after my prayer, Nellie Jo called again: "The JV game went into overtime. Our guys had it won, but the other team came back in the last minute."

Thank God for a good opponent.

It would still be close, but now I had a chance. I made it to the school, ran into the gym. Within minutes the introduction was made: "Ladies and gentlemen, senior Art Rainer is accompanied by his mother *and* father, Dr. and Mrs. Thom Rainer." Art smiled at me and said with confidence, "Glad you made it Dad. I knew you would."

THE SECRETS OF SUCCESS OF A WORKAHOLIC AND DISTRACTED DAD

I need to make a point abundantly clear here. In many ways I am portrayed as a hero, a super dad in this book. And you have heard me say that sometimes I do OK, but often I have failed miserably. On those occasions when I did succeed, I could see a common factor summed up in two words: Nellie Jo.

My wife coordinated all of my boys' activities with my assistant to make certain that they got on my calendar. She reminded me what time I needed to be home for us to make games and other activities. She gently persisted in making certain that I would not miss some key moments in my boys' lives that I would live to regret.

In many ways, I gave my boys quantity and quality time because my wife made certain that I did. She showed greater wisdom, greater discernment, and more sacrificial love than I ever did. She is the true hero. This should be her book.

When a Father Says Good-bye

I had the rare opportunity to sit with my father during his last days on earth. I must admit that I felt rushed. There was so much I wanted to talk about before he was no longer able to communicate with me. Those days were precious, but he died with so much left to say.

You have heard me say a lot about my dad in this book. I think I have been too hard on him. He was a great dad, and he loved me dearly. He worked hard for our family. I learned so much from him.

The issues I have raised have been my heartfelt desires to spend more time with him, to talk with and to be encouraged by him. I never doubted his love or approval; I just longed to hear it. So when he died, I was left longing. Our best conversations as father and son did not really begin until days before his death.

And even today, I long for more time with my dad.

There is the likelihood that my three sons will tell me good-bye. I do not want to leave this life with my boys left wanting.

When the final chapters of my life are written, I will not be best remembered as a speaker. Few people will recall the hundreds of events where I spoke.

I will not be best remembered as a writer. None of my books made the best-seller's list.

I will not be remembered first as a denominational leader, a role I never expected to occupy anyway.

But the legacy I leave are three sons. They are Art, Jess, and Sam.

I have messed up many times, but I hope they will know that I was there for them.

I hope they will know that I was always eager to talk to them.

I hope they will say that I voiced my approval of them and pride in them again and again.

I hope they will know that I loved them, and that I *said* that I loved them.

And I hope they will say that I gave them the gift of time.

Then, and only then, will I be at peace that I have not lived my life in vain.

Chapter 9

The Transparent Father

As you can tell from earlier chapters, I moved several times during my childhood. Because my dad was unwilling to compromise God's calling on his life, our family moved six times in my first eighteen years of life. Before I dive into the next story, I want you, the reader, to take a mental note that even with all of the difficulty that comes with moving, I do not look back on the uprooting of our lives as a negative, but as positive. I have come to view these moves as one long road trip on which I met numerous people and made countless memories. Looking back, it is clear that God has been with our family all the way. He had, and still does have, a plan for each of our lives. Now, having said that, allow me to tell you about a very important moment in my life.

The school year had come to an end. I had just finished the sixth grade, and nothing but the glorious days of summer lay ahead. As most people can relate, there was a certain feeling in the air that meant little league baseball games, jumping off the high dive at the neighborhood pool, flirting with the girls, pick-up football games, family vacations, and visiting grandparents. Freedom from teachers, homework, and the pressure of grades. It was both a unique and beautiful time in my life. There was nothing and everything to do, all at the same time.

As I eagerly left the school building in Birmingham, Alabama, I did not realize that it would be my last day at that particular school. Up until this moment, my family had lived in the city for four years, the longest stint of my life to date. I had made incredible friends. Jay, Kipp, David, Bobby, Preston, and Patrick—now just pictures in an old yearbook—had become my elementary school confidants. We spent the night at each other's houses, played sports together, crashed birthday parties, and told each other of our girlfriend crushes. During those years, I could not have asked for better friends. I felt that I belonged. My life was good and I enjoyed it greatly, and since the school included all grades, from kindergarten to twelfth, I expected to spend many more years with these guys. Nothing was going to break us.

I even remember talking to my dad one day about moving to another place prior to this summer. He had been offered a pastoral position at a church in San Diego, California, and declined the offer. He told me that he could not see himself living anywhere else. He was in God's will and felt that we would stay in Birmingham for many years, and that made my young heart happy.

"Good. I don't want to move anywhere else," I said.

"Me neither," he replied.

But all of these ideals quickly vanished in the summer between my sixth and seventh grade years. Dad was asked to start a new graduate school of missions and evangelism at a seminary in Louisville. The opportunity was incredible, and little did I realize (mainly out of my refusal to accept it as fact) how seriously he was looking into accepting the position. God had turned his comfort into uneasiness and changed his rock-solid decision to stay a pastor in Alabama into a pile of rubble. He had a new calling for his life and had to follow it.

One afternoon that summer, my dad and mom asked me to come into the kitchen where both of them sat at the table solemnly. I sat down across from my dad. My mom was beside me, at the front of the table.

"Son," my dad said. "You know about the job that has been offered to me in Louisville?"

"Yeah."

"Well, I think that God is telling me that I need to take that position."

"Does that mean that we will have to move?" I said, fearing the answer that I already knew.

"I am afraid so, Art."

There was a brief moment where no one said anything, and then the tears started overflowing my eyes, traveling down my cheeks.

Struggling to speak because of the tremendous lump in my throat, I said, "But I don't want to go."

"I know," was all that he could say, for tears had started gathering in his eyes as well. As I buried my head in my arms on the table to hide the flood that was about to be released from my eyes, he did something that I will never forget. He cried.

You can tell when someone's tears are real, truly rooted in some heartfelt emotion. Dad's tears were genuine. There was meaning behind them. They came from deep within. It was amazing. He just sat there at the kitchen table, mourning, as if I were the one telling him that he had to move. For a while, we just sat together and cried. There was nothing else that needed to be said. He put aside any façade of being the strong, mighty father and showed all his emotions and thoughts in a single moment. Through this, I realized that he was just like me—sad and no longer certain of the future.

In that moment, everything was *not* all right, and there was no need to act as if it were. Dad unashamedly became transparent in front of me, which was exactly what I needed while sitting at that table. No hug, consoling, or words of encouragement could have helped me more than seeing my father truly relate to the same feelings and emotions that weighed on my heart as well.

He hurt because I hurt. He cried because I cried. At that moment I knew he cared how I felt, and that the decision he had made was not easy.

Transparency makes everything clear and obvious. To be transparent is to put one's life in full view. There are no hidden secrets. Flaws can be seen; mistakes are made known. Transparency does not allow for perfection and, at times, can be terrifying. Yet at the same time, it is biblical, and for the bold who choose to pursue this crazy way of life, it can be fulfilling. Through his emotions, heart, mind, and soul, my dad maintained an undeniable transparency that continues to strengthen our relationship into the depths that we share today.

EMOTIONAL TRANSPARENCY

From the previous story, it is clear how my father was transparent with his emotions. Now for most guys, this becomes a difficult issue to address. Showing our emotions, especially when it includes crying, is not considered masculine in our culture. In a guy's world, those who are able to hold back the tears are considered the stronger, better men.

To be completely honest, I struggle with the same issue; it is definitely a guy thing. (If you happen to be a woman reading this part, please bear with me. As you probably know, we guys operate a little differently, and showing our emotions does not come easily to us.) Now, I am not going to make this brief section a counseling session for men and their emotional issues, but I can tell you about a guy—my dad—who showed his emotions without compromising his manhood during my childhood.

Whether it was extreme happiness or deep sadness, my father was unafraid to share his emotions. He would jump with excitement anytime something good happened to his sons, and he would let the tears flow when he discussed the love of his wife. He laid his cards out on the table so that everyone could see what he was experiencing, yet he did it in a way that left no question about his masculinity. His emotions were honest, and he shared them with others.

Seeing this as a child impacted me greatly. I am still more stoic than my father, but I realize that because of his emotional transparency, I was able to connect more easily with him. I now understand that I was able to share any emotions that flowed through my heart with my father because I knew that he could relate to those same feelings. I had seen it firsthand. This created a closer bond between father and son as we shared in each other's lives.

TRANSPARENCY OF THE HEART

The love, care, and passion for the family that exuded from my father's heart could not be anything but transparent. I have already touched on the fact that I never had to question my father's love for me, and I only hope that every child could come to the same realization that I did as a kid. Too many men let their children grow up before they realize that they never showed their kids how much they really loved them, that they would probably give up their lives for their children. Crucial time passes, and it becomes too late. As life moves on, so do the children, and the damage is done.

For my father, the words "I love you" could not come out of his mouth enough times during the course of a day. He openly professed his love for his sons and for his beloved wife. His heart was openly pounding for his family.

This transparency was not seen only by the family. Everywhere he went and with whomever he came into contact, it was clear and obvious—he loved his family. We were his passion; his heart's desire. That love could be seen in his face and reflected in the excitement of his voice whenever he talked about us. From my child's-eye view, only his relationship with God seemed to come before his deep, devotional love for our family. As a growing child, I knew that I held a special place in my dad's heart. How did I know?

He was transparent.

MENTAL TRANSPARENCY

"AWFUL CALL, REF!"

"FOUL!"

"THROW THE FLAG! THROW THE FLAG!"

"HE ELBOWED HIM!"

"THEY'RE PLAYING DIRTY, REF!"

"HOLD! HOLD!"

"THAT WAS PATHETIC, REF! JUST PATHETIC!"

You could hear his yell from across the football field. His fury could be felt in any high school basketball gym. Refs knew him by name—and not because they asked. Home and visitor fans alike had no doubt at any time during an athletic event what was on his mind. That was my dad.

I am not suggesting that any parent act as my father did at my brothers' and my sporting events. In fact, you all should probably do quite the opposite. But at our games, he was passionate. As far as he was concerned, whatever was on his mind should be out there for the rest of those attending to hear.

Outside of the sporting arena, my dad was very good at letting his family know what was on his mind. He did not try to hide anything from us. He would never tell us a lie in order to "protect" us from the truth. (Needless to say, I found out about Santa very early in my life.) We never had to guess what he was thinking. Some may say that this can be hazardous to relationships, but for me it fostered trust in my father.

I could come to him with any question and get an honest answer, even when the truth was not what I wanted to hear. This is the primary reason why he is still the major sounding board which I bounce ideas off. On any issue, I know that his thoughts will be truthful, transparent.

TRANSPARENCY OF THE SOUL

My dad followed God. He wore this on his sleeve more than any other aspect of his life. His relationship with the Creator came first and foremost in his life. Before any dream, any desire, and even any family member, my dad's soul belongs to Christ. Through almost every action taken and every decision made by my dad, God's leading was the influence that took precedence over everything else, and this still holds true today as it did while I was in my youth.

This transparency of the soul shaped not only how I view my father, but it also serves as a model for my relationship with God. Out of all of the areas that were transparent in Dad's life, this was by far the most important.

If you take away his pastoring, teaching, writing, and consulting, God is still unmistakably the driver of his life. God is as much a part of his home life as any other element in his life. He loves his Creator without hesitation or regard for others' opinions. He is living to impress only one, the One.

I really don't know what is more important than spiritual transparency. Throughout my life Dad has been one of my most important spiritual role models. His relationship with Christ is so evident; I can only hope to achieve the same bond with God that he had. I proudly state that this is the most passionate aspect of his life. In an age when spiritual transparency is considered offensive, he stands to offend.

I am grateful for my dad's transparencies. Because of these, I know him well.

That should be something that every child can say.

And it is the blessing I take into my own family.

— A Father's Perspective —

Please allow me to take a pause from the usual pattern of these chapters and say something about the approach Art and I used in this book. From a content point of view, he pretty much determined the path that we would take. He would always write the first half of the chapter without any input from me. Art wanted and received complete freedom to shape this project.

But that occasionally means that what he writes brings me discomfort.

Why did he have to tell my deep dark secrets about the referees?

Yes, I am competitive. And yes, I did on occasion *encourage* the referees. But I only did so seven or eight times a game. And I only did so for some twenty years.

OK, I was a jerk.

But I really got into my sons' games. Still, it is painful to hear Art recalling those times for which I gained notoriety.

I repent. At least until the grandchildren start playing.

HONEST TEARS

Without a doubt, writing this book has been one of the great joys of my life and, paradoxically, a very painful experience as well. When I read how Art views me and looks up to me, I consider myself one of the most blessed men in the world. The weekend before I wrote this chapter, I had the opportunity to spend time with each of my boys, no small feat since we live in four separate cities.

Sam wanted to talk about some ministry opportunities at his church, and about his dream to become a leading Christian researcher.

Art talked with me about some of his dreams for ministry, and how he hopes that will come to fruition.

Jess spoke with me about some deep spiritual issues until 2:30 in the morning.

I love talking to my sons. I love being with my sons. And I will tell anyone who will listen how much I love them. There is no doubt that I am totally transparent about my love and commitment to my sons.

Not only am I transparent *about* my sons, I am transparent *with* my sons. Though I have tried not to overreact emotionally, my three sons have seen my tears on occasion.

They saw me cry at each of their baptisms.

They saw me cry when my mother died.

They saw me cry when we received the diagnosis that Nellie Jo's cancer had spread.

And they saw me cry when they presented me with a video tribute for my fiftieth birthday.

The tears that I have shed have been honest tears.

Art told the story of my crying when he was so broken-hearted about leaving his home and friends in Birmingham. I know I cried first because of the pain I saw in my son's face and in his words. But I also cried because I saw the possibility that I was sacrificing my family for my own career. I thought it was God's will for us to move, but I do not have perfect discernment. So the tears came.

Honest tears.

Transparency.

Sometimes transparency is good.

But sometimes it is not.

THE PROBLEM WITH TRANSPARENCY

Art commented earlier that I have always been very open with my sons. Such a posture may have some advantages, but there are definitely disadvantages. While I want to have an open relationship with my sons, there are times when it is best for a parent to keep matters to himself or herself. I failed several times to remember my own admonitions.

Though the examples are probably in great numbers, the failure I remember most clearly was a few years where I served at a particular church. I was pastor of four churches when the boys were growing up. All the churches were blessings, and I am thankful for the time I spent with each of them.

But of the four churches, one was much more difficult than the others. I am not assigning blame to anyone or any church; I know I share in the blame. But I would be less than honest if I did not say that one of the four churches was my least joyful experience.

The critics were vocal in that church. It seemed that I was being second-guessed on every leadership decision I made. And a few of the members were downright mean to me. I would sometimes hear accusations made about me that I knew were totally unfounded.

Now a good father would share his wounds in the privacy of a room with his wife, and even then he would be circumspect about not always being negative around her. And a good father definitely would not bring his sons in on the woes created by members of that church.

But I did.

I would whine to my three boys about what this person said and what that person did. I would share with them the painful experiences of some contentious church business meetings.

I was dead wrong in my transparency here.

Those three boys did not need to know every little negative issue about that church. And though they do not seem to be bitter about the church today, I obviously biased them negatively toward people and issues in the church. Even as adults today, the boys will mention certain antagonists in that church, though many years have passed.

A good father would have kept those issues to himself. A good father would not have felt the need to share his pain with three young sons. A good father would have been more stoic and would have realized that transparency is not always good.

I was not a good father in this regard. I really blew it.

And the fact of the matter is, the problems were probably never as great as they seemed. So not only did I prejudice my sons against a church and some of the members (would *poison* be too strong a word?), I undoubtedly overstated the pain.

I blew it. Transparency is not always good.

THE JOYS OF TRANSPARENCY

OK, I have been hard on myself. I deserve it.

But more times than not, I was transparent for the right reasons. Let me share with you four of those reasons.

First, I have always been transparent in my love for my sons. Art has made this point abundantly clear throughout this book and, at least in this instance, I agree with him fully. The spoken and unequivocal love of a father is a blessing, a blessing that I pray they will give to their own children.

I have always told my boys that I loved them whenever they have experienced success in life. Jess called me to tell me that he earned another 4.0 at college and he will likely graduate with highest honors. I told him that I was proud of him and that I loved him. Art boldly made appointments with some leading businessmen in the nation to share some of his dreams and to get some input from them. I told him that I was proud of his boldness and that I loved him. Sam shared with me a major research project that received accolades from many. I told him how incredible the project was and how much I loved him.

But I don't express my love for the boys only when they do well. I love them even when they blow it, and I tell them so.

I fear that readers of this book will get the impression that Art and I are attempting to portray the Rainer family as *the* super family in America. I hope you have heard otherwise. I am far from perfect, and so are my boys.

When Art called me from his summer mission trip in San Diego, he was, by his own admission, very nervous. He had heard his dad say all of his life what a great son he was. He had a great security and a great joy in knowing that his dad thought so highly of him. But he was worried. He worried and wondered. Will Dad no longer think so well of me? Will he not brag on me as he has done for so many years?

When Art shared his two years of less-than-perfect living at college with me, I could almost hear him swallowing hard by telephone more than two thousand miles away. The moment of truth had arrived.

As we shared earlier, I did not condone his behavior, but I quickly told him of my forgiveness and unconditional love. I was still proud of my son. I still loved him immeasurably. You could almost hear the long-distance sigh of relief.

Transparency is good when we are unashamedly and unreservedly telling our children we love them. In good times and bad.

And by the way, I also tell my boys I love them just to tell them I love them. There doesn't have to be a positive or negative occasion to do so. I just like to be open with them and express my heart and emotions.

A second positive aspect of transparency is that my boys rarely had doubts on where I stood on any issue. They knew they were doing something wrong *before* they ever did anything wrong. They most always knew my sentiments on something before they ever asked me.

My boys simply know me well. And they tell me that there is a certain comfort and security in knowing my position and feelings. Transparency is good there.

A related and third positive aspect of transparency is the removal of the fear of the unknown. I received a call from Nellie Jo while I was involved in a church consultation in North Carolina. She told me that our oldest son, Sam, had a sizeable lump in his neck. The doctor had scheduled a biopsy for as soon as possible.

I was devastated. I caught the quickest flight back home that I could. I went to my son's room and talked with him and prayed with him. I let him know that, while I was upset, we were going to find out all we could about this situation, and we were going to trust God to take care of it.

I then spent the rest of the night on the Internet. (Yeah, I know, it's not always wise to be an Internet physician.) I looked at as many possibilities as I could find and shared them with Sam the next day. I told him that even in the event of a malignancy, these problems are rarely fatal. He seemed greatly relieved with my open approach to his situation, and he entered the biopsy procedures with courage and confidence.

The good news is that the lump was benign. Sam goes to his physician to have it checked every six months. In this situation, transparency was good.

A fourth benefit of my transparency with my sons is that it has brought us closer together. We share things with one another that are private and deep. There are not too many subjects that are off limits for us. As a result, we have bonded even closer together as father and sons. Transparency can be good.

I would like to end the chapter here, but I can't.

Integrity demands that I respond to Art's comments on my transparent relationship with God. This too shall be painful for me.

ANOTHER PAINFUL REMINDER

In the early part of this chapter, Art wrote these words: *"Throughout my life Dad has been one of my most important spiritual role models. His relationship with Christ is so evident, I can only hope to achieve the same bond with God that he has. I proudly state that this is the most passionate aspect of his life. In an age where spiritual transparency is considered offensive, he stands to offend."*

To see Art's perspective, you might get the impression that I am Charles Spurgeon, George Whitefield, John Hyde,

Martin Luther, and the apostle Paul synthesized as one. But sadly, I know my failures.

I was consistent in reading the Bible with the boys when they were young. I was inconsistent in having Bible studies with the boys when they were older.

I was consistent in preaching about the power of prayer, and I did pray with my sons regularly. But I was inconsistent in my prayer life with my wife. I was not a good role model for them to pray with their wives.

I was consistent in speaking and writing about the need to share our faith with others. But I was inconsistent in witnessing. Sometimes my busyness confused my priorities.

I was consistent in knowing doctrinal truths well. But I was inconsistent in that my boys did not always see me live out those truths.

Transparency in my relationship with God? Well, I am glad Art saw the best side of me there and followed those positive examples. From my perspective, I failed many times. In my estimation, he could have just as easily written about a father who was often hypocritical in his walk with God.

I preach it and teach it far better than I practice it.

Thank God for His grace.

And the grace of my sons.

Chapter 10

A Time to Let Go

Ah, fraternity life!

The parties. The girls. The drinking. The lack of responsibility. The lack of class attendance. The stupid charades. The laziness. The drugs. The hazing. The drinking. The bars. The late nights. The happenings at the fraternity house. The alcohol. The smoking. The girls at the parties. The drinking. The drinking.

Such are the stereotypes that both Christians and non-Christians have about the life of fraternity members. The world portrays fraternity life as a life without care or regard for anyone or anything. It is all about me, myself, and I. There is no other focus than self, and personal gratification is the only thing that matters. Whereas fraternities were originally created to provide a gateway for boys to become men and to learn valuable life lessons, now they are perceived to exist only for debauchery.

So when I called my father to ask if he would mind that I join a fraternity on campus, I expected the worst. How could the prestigious Dr. Rainer have a son who was a member of one of these "evil" brotherhoods? He was already well respected for the rearing of his three sons, and if he allowed his son to become a fraternity member, he could lose credibility among his peers. However, much to my amazement, he said that I could if I wanted to join. He let me make a decision that would impact me for the rest of my life. I was allowed to open my eyes and see the world as it is and not some fictitious picture that would leave me naïve.

My dad was very good at this. He never wanted my brothers and me to be the overprotected children who could not see beyond their own home. He wanted us to experience the world and all of the realities that come with it. For this, I am grateful, and my transition to life after parents has been easy because my father did not let us leave the nest in ignorance. He protected his sons by allowing us to know the world in full, with all of the good and bad it offers.

MAKING OUR OWN DECISIONS

Photographs are great. They bring back many memories that would have otherwise gone forgotten. Sometimes this is a good thing, and other times, those memories are best left alone. If you were to go through some of the Rainer family pictures, you would find some absolutely hilarious photos. The most laughable pictures are always those that show off our personal preference in attire, especially those taken during the 1980s and early 1990s. What were we thinking!

I was thumbing through a few stacks of photos the other day at my parents' house, and I could not help but laugh when I saw my dad with shorts so short that I could not help but blurt out "Whoa!" while cringing and holding the picture as far from my eyes as possible. It was like watching one of those surgeries on television—you don't want to look, but for some reason, the sheer disgust of it leaves you in a trance, staring. After the initial shock, the laughter came freely.

Continuing to look through the stack, I ran across a picture of my older brother during his "nerd" days. This kid looked goofy. He had HUGE glasses that covered most of his face, and he wore a neon pink tank top. Of course we can't ignore the half bottle of hair spray that was holding up his bangs to look like the bill of a hat. It was weird!

The funniest pictures, however, were of my little brother, Jess. You can see *them* in almost all of his pictures as a child. Where there is Jess, *they* are there as well. What exactly am I talking about? Bright neon socks. He loved them all. Neon pink, neon green, and neon blue. If they were neon and fit on his feet, he wore them. They stood out like a sore thumb. They looked like an accident, but unfortunately they weren't.

After seeing these pictures, I had to ask my parents, "Why did you let us wear this stuff? We looked like clowns back then!"

My parents' response: "You wanted to wear that stuff. We let you make your own choices."

"Maybe you should have stepped in on this one," I replied, and we all had a good laugh.

That brief conversation got me thinking about my childhood and the decisions my parents allowed me to make. From the clothes I wore to the sports I played to the girls I dated to the faith I followed, I made my life's decisions. This was my life through and through, not theirs. Granted, my choices were greatly influenced by my parents' presence in my upbringing, but I have no doubt that who I am today is a result of my own personal decisions.

Now I should be clear: our parents did not give us carte blanche in making decisions in our lives. There were boundaries. But the older we got, the more responsibility and freedom they gave us.

I remember when I wanted to change schools my freshman year of high school. For some reason, maybe through the influence of my friends who went to public school, I wanted to leave my private, Christian school and attend a local public school. It just seemed "cooler" than my school. When I told my parents, I expected a negative reaction to their "ungrateful" son. I braced myself. However, they did not respond as I feared. They just looked at me and said, "Well, give it a couple weeks and think about it. If you still want to transfer, you can go." Shocked that the decision lay in my hands, I left the room to go think. I decided not to transfer, and over the course of my high school years, I made some of the best friends that I have ever had. This was probably what they wanted for me, but they let it be my choice.

It was very important to me that I was able to make my own decisions while still under my parents' watch. I see too many children today who seem to be over-parented. From very early on in their lives, they are told what activities to do, who to have "play dates" with, and where they need to go. Their lives are completely structured by their parents. They have no room to make their own decisions and find out who they really are. It's scary and sad at the same time. Where is the excitement in this? Where is the real life? What will happen to these children when they must get out on their own?

Making my own choices allowed me to make mistakes. My parents were not afraid to allow my brothers and me to make mistakes (hence, the neon socks). I have made countless mistakes in my life, and each has served as an essential tool to my understanding of this life that God has given me. I learn more from the blunders in my life than from the correct choices. For some reason, the errors seem to stick longer in my mind and have more of an impact on future decisions than the right answers. I can only speak for myself on this, but I love my mistakes. Sure, they initially hurt or made me feel like an idiot, but the lasting impact has been so great, I could not imagine my life without them.

Thank you, Mom and Dad, for giving me no one but myself to blame for the mistakes I made. You provided the influence but left the decision up to me. Thank you for the numerous life lessons that this taught me, lessons that I could have missed.

UNDERSTANDING THE VALUE OF A LITTLE SWEAT

Life is not easy. We know this because we live it. Rarely is anything obtained, small or large, in our lives that did not cause us to work a little. No goal or dream is achieved without the sweat of someone. The majority of the world works this way. Especially here in the United States, those who put forth more effort than others around them will achieve more, or so the dream goes. Greatness is a burden that is placed on the backs of those who are willing to carry it to its destination.

I am still amazed when I run across children whose parents give them an allowance for nothing—literally. No making the bed, no putting up the toys, no helping Mom and Dad with the dishes. They just reach out their hands at the end of the week, and money is given to them. What is the lesson learned here? Ask and you shall receive! I don't think this is what Jesus had in mind when He said this.

Dad made sure that we worked for our money. Every week my brothers and I had a list of chores given to us. During the summer it seemed that we were given a list of chores every day, though that may be an exaggeration. I hated chores. Back then, they seemed like such a pain. I would read down the list:

Chore 1: Dust the entire den. *AAAAGH!*
Chore 2: Vacuum living room. *The agony!*
Chore 3: Mop kitchen floor. *Why me??*
Chore 4: Sweep front porch. *My life is over!*

When we were young, these were incredibly daunting tasks. And in return, we received a quarter for every chore completed. Except for convincing my younger brother, Jess, that a shiny penny was worth more than a quarter, these chores were my only source of income when I was a youth. If I wanted to buy a new action figure, I would either have to do more chores or wait till Christmas or my birthday, whichever came first.

Though, at the time, I thought of these chores as God's curse on mankind, they allowed me to learn the value of working early on in my life. I became acquainted with the feeling of satisfaction that comes from an accomplishment created by a little sweat on the brow. These early lessons have become a mind-set for me. I understand that I cannot expect anything other than God's grace to be given to me in this life. There are no guarantees, and I must be willing to put forth extra effort to fulfill any dreams that I may have. The day that I think otherwise is the day that I become lazy. Work is a reality, and I must look at it as such. I am very fortunate to have a dad who instilled this idea in my life.

THE NAKED TRUTH

As I have already touched on in the previous chapter, my dad was truthful. He was never one to hide or water down the reality of a matter in order to protect his children from the real world. In every situation, he presented the truth to us as if he were talking to a friend. If he felt that we did not understand everything he was saying, he would not hesitate to explain it to us. Growing up, I never felt that my dad was hiding something from me. Whether it was one of my questions on sex, AIDS, murder, or war, my father would explain these issues in the best way he knew how.

I never heard my dad say, "You are too young for me to talk to you about this. When you get older, I will explain everything." He never backed down. Though I imagine this was not easy for my father, he was ready and willing to share the reality of any circumstance or topic.

NOT TOO REAL

Now you may be reading this and thinking, *Well, why didn't he just go ahead and throw you out on the street and let you fend for yourself? The more "real" the better, right? You can't get much more "real" than that.* While there may be some validity to that statement, I don't recommend anyone do that to a child.

My father made sure that my brothers and I were prepared to enter the real world when we left our parents' care. During the preparation period, everything he did, he did in love. He never purposefully neglected us in the name of preparation. Children need to feel protected, and my father was definitely there to protect us when life necessitated. I knew that I could run to him in a time of need. I had quite a few nightmares as a kid, and I knew that if I had a bad dream, I could run to my parents' room and be safe. In their room, nightmares were not allowed.

I included this chapter in the book to speak to those parents who are overprotecting their children. It is those children for whom I have concern when they leave the home of their parents and must take care of themselves. There must be a balance of protection and reality that is given to the youth. As I have already mentioned, I am forever grateful because my father allowed me to experience the world and understand its happenings before I left my parents' supervision.

By the way, joining a fraternity became a tremendous turning point in my life. I experienced God's grace more than ever before, and it solidified a walk with Christ that I would not give up for life itself.

Good choice.

— A Father's Perspective —

It is never easy. To hear Art's perspective, you might get the impression that I had the wisdom of Solomon, that I could make immediate and profound decisions regarding my sons.

Wrong.

I really did struggle about how much freedom I should give my sons. I did not have a neat chart that detailed at what point certain freedoms should be dispensed. It just wasn't that easy.

The fraternity decision was a struggle for me. I had been in a fraternity in a state school, so I knew the downside of allowing Art to join. While I know that a lot can change in twenty-three years, I also know that much remains the same. Art had been in the relatively protected environment of a Christian school for almost all of his childhood. I knew the transition to a state school *and* a fraternity would be dramatic, if not traumatic.

Where is the rulebook for fatherhood anyway?

It is fascinating to hear Art's understanding of events *ex post facto*. I never made the decision to allow him to change schools. I simply did not make a decision at all. Frankly, I was unsure if I would let him move, but I did not want to make a hasty decision one way or the other. Art's view is that I gave tacit permission for him to transfer schools. My perspective is that I was totally confused. It all worked out because he came to the conclusion on his own that he would not move.

But Art didn't mention the boom boxes.

And I think he left out that story because it did not involve him, but it did involve his two brothers. Those infernal boom boxes.

I know that there is a more accurate name for boom boxes, but I know them by their acoustical nomenclature. I am referring to those big boxes you put in cars. They amplify the bass in songs via the radio or CD player. In fact, the bass is so loud that you can rarely understand the song.

Not only are boom boxes loud, they take up valuable storage space in the car. They are some of the most worthless pieces of equipment I have ever known.

I hate boom boxes.

BOOM. BOOM. BABOOM. BABOOM. BOOM. BOOM.

I hate boom boxes.

My oldest son Sam was the first child to test me on this putrid piece of equipment.

"Absolutely not, son. Those things are so loud that they disturb the whole neighborhood."

"Dad, I promise I will keep the volume low and not disturb anyone."

"No way, you will tear up your car trying to install it."

"No, Dad. There is a professional installer just three miles away."

"Forget it, son; those things are just too expensive."

"But Dad, you promised us that we could buy things we wanted if we paid for it with our own earned money."

Sigh.

You guessed it. I gave in.

And you know what? Both Sam and Jess kept every promise they made about the boom boxes. Fortunately, they soon outgrew the desire to keep those disgusting and demented contraptions.

I still hate boom boxes.

RESPONSIBILITY AND FREEDOM

I tried to be consistent in deciding when to give my sons new freedoms. While I know I fell short many times, I did have certain guidelines that I followed. My wife, though stricter than I, joined me in following four basic principles.

Principle 1: Discern If the Issue Is One of Preference or Moral Responsibility

It never happened this way, but if one of my teenage boys told me that they wanted to go bar-hopping and engage in underage drinking, the decision would have been easy: absolutely not!

The three boys never knowingly put us in a position where they asked us for permission to engage in some unbiblical or immoral behaviors. But there were times when they pushed the envelope.

Jess, our youngest son, loves fireworks. I was once worried that he had pyromaniacal tendencies. South of Nashville off of I-65 is a huge fireworks store called Sad Sam's. Whenever we would approach the store, Jess would begin his routine of puppy-dog begging.

"Please stop, Dad. I will use my own money. I will never ask for anything again. This is the most important thing in my life."

I yielded again.

And I had grounds to be uncomfortable. Some of the clerks were missing fingers. Some of the packages had stern warnings on them: "Exploding these fireworks may precipitate such a violent reaction that you may be responsible for World War III."

OK, I exaggerated. Except about the part about the missing fingers.

One time we arrived at Cape San Blas, Florida, with sufficient explosives to launch a space shuttle. Jess could not wait. Unfortunately, a note had been left in our condo: "Due to drought conditions, it is prohibited by law to use fireworks on Cape San Blas."

I showed the note to Jess.

"But Dad, I can send the fireworks over the ocean. There is no way they can start a fire."

But the law was the law. His protests were in vain. He remained a disappointed boy on this vacation.

The teachable moment came when law enforcement officers came to the beach to give citations to all who were participating in the lighting of fireworks. Lesson learned.

Still. I must admit that I never got it exactly right. On many occasions I said no to a son's request just because I didn't like it. Not because it was wrong. Not because it was illegal or immoral. Just because I didn't like it. It was not my personal preference.

Where are instruction books on being a father?

Principle 2: Overcome the Desire to Be a Control Freak

He was one of the most successful boys in high school. He excelled in academics. He was an outstanding athlete. He had a great personality. He had natural leadership abilities. And he was good looking, a prime target for the girls in our class.

I don't know where he is today. The last I heard he had experienced failed marriages, psychological meltdown, and a career collapse. Someone told me he was an unkempt taxi driver in a large city.

Now I must be very careful at this point. I do not know the hearts and issues of other people. I have enough trouble dealing with my own issues. But many of us predicted it about my friend. We could see it coming. His father was an absolute control freak.

I went to his home one day. My friend was not allowed to communicate with me in any fashion until he had completed his minimum two hours a day of study. His father made me sit in another room and wait for the remaining twenty minutes of his time.

He had to practice a musical instrument. He had to be involved in at least two sports. He had to be at the top of his class academically.

Anything and everything was reviewed and approved by his father. None of us were thus surprised when my friend did not know how to handle freedom outside the constant watch of his father. He had a complete and total meltdown.

My parents were not strict disciplinarians when I was a teenager. The clear boundaries of my early childhood became muddled in my teen years. It seemed that Mom and Dad simply did not want to fight the battles that come with maintaining discipline with a teenager. But I sure wish they had. My rebellious behavior was often a cry for greater involvement and greater discipline by my parents.

The balance is difficult. And I know I failed too often. I was too strict at times with my oldest son, Sam. I was too lenient at times with my youngest son, Jess. And don't think for a minute that I got it just right with Art, the middle son.

And after twenty-seven years of raising three sons, I still did not always get it right. When Jess, the youngest, was about to graduate from college, he wanted to go on a road trip by himself to Telluride, Colorado. You know what my reaction was? Overprotection. Controlling. I had so many reasons why he shouldn't go. But he was a twenty-two-year-old man. It was time to let go. But that is the subject of the end of this chapter.

Principle 3: Increasing Responsibility, Increasing Freedom

"Why does Sam get to stay up to 10:30? It's not fair!" I cannot count how many times I heard that statement of indignation: "It's not fair!" More often than not, the statement was made from one of the younger brothers. Since there is a five-year age difference between the youngest and the oldest child, the lack of fairness seemed easily apparent to the child who had the least number of privileges.

Nellie Jo and I were fairly consistent in our philosophy. The older you got, the more responsibilities you had. And if you handled your responsibilities well, you had more privileges.

That is why our boys had to earn their money, even at very young ages. We were teaching our sons responsibility. And when those responsibilities were handled well, you earned a later bed time. Or you could spend an extra night at a friend's house. Or you could earn a trip to the toy store (the destination changed, of course, with age). Or you could watch one extra hour of television.

But the moment a responsibility was not carried out, we attempted immediately to remove freedoms. As older teens, two of our sons experienced this reality with the same painful lessons. Because they did not do as they were told, we took their driving privileges from them. They could not drive a car for two weeks. They could only ride with us or with older adults. They could not even be in a car if a friend was driving.

The experiences of two of the sons were separated by two years, but both boys got the message. One of the sons could only go on a date with his girlfriend if Nellie Jo or I or the girlfriend's parents drove.

We never had a problem with that issue again.

Though I was not perfect, I think I was more consistent than not. The prayerful goal of Nellie Jo and me was to move our sons deliberately toward adulthood. We didn't want to push so hard that our children did not enjoy their childhood. But we wanted to push sufficiently that they were prepared for adulthood.

The ultimate test of our theory came when the boys left the comfortable nest of their parents' home and started their own. How would we do when we finally let go?

Principle 4: Finally Letting Go

All three sons are married now. All have their own homes. All are independent. I will talk about their wives in the conclusion of this book. For now, let me address the issue of letting go.

In our prayer times together, Nellie Jo and I have had a consistent prayer. First, we prayed that all three sons would come to a point where they received Jesus Christ as their Lord and Savior. Our greatest and most fervent prayers were for their eternities.

Our second most common prayer was for God to provide our boys with godly wives. We have been blessed with answers to both prayers. Our sons are outstanding Christian men with wonderful Christian wives.

You see, our prayer life has been a key and integral part of the process of letting go. We first wanted to let them go into the forgiving and loving hands of a Savior who loved them more than we. We wanted them to have the assurance of Jesus' love more than anything else.

Then we wanted them to experience the joy of starting their own families. We wanted them to leave the home of Thom and Nellie Jo Rainer and start new homes and new families. We wanted to let go.

When our boys' wedding days came, Nellie Jo and I were not the least bit sad. We had been preparing for that day all of the boys' lives. But more than preparing for it, we were praying for it. So those three weddings were clear answers to our prayers.

Art was the first of the three to get married. And when he joined hands at the front of the church with his beautiful bride, Sarah, I moved next to them and said a prayer as I put my hand on my son's shoulder.

I don't remember the details of the prayer fully. I do remember thanking God for the gift of joy He gave us in Art. And I remember praising God for the great daughter-in-law we were receiving. My prayer also included a prayer of thanksgiving for the salvation of both Art and Sarah. I concluded the prayer and then sat down next to Nellie Jo.

No one saw it. At least I don't think they did.

The tears fell quickly but profusely.

They were unexpected—but they were not accompanied with sadness.

That was my baby getting married. That was the little fellow that kept us in stitches with his one-liners. That was the son who loved to talk with his dad about matters of sports, theology, business, and girlfriends.

That was my son.

I was letting go. His primary family would now be with Sarah and, God willing, the children they bring into this world.

It was a strange feeling—but it was right.

"For this reason a man will leave his father and mother and be joined to his wife, and the two will become one flesh[.] . . . Therefore what God has joined together, man must not separate" (Matt. 19:5–6).

I let go.

God is good.

Chapter 11

~~~~~~~~

Evolution of a Dad

As I reminisce about the years gone by with my dad, it is clear that our relationship has changed significantly. The change is not negative; I am just pointing out the obvious.

As people change over time, the relationships between people do as well. Some of our relationships grow ever deeper with time while others diminish till there is almost nothing left. Once close friends become distant, and casual acquaintances become best friends. This is the nature of relationships; rarely do they remain stagnant.

Who my dad was and who I was during my middle school years is drastically different from who we are now. Though I remain the same in name and genetics, I am not the toddler my dad once sat in his lap. Dad has become wiser with his age, and I have hopefully matured a little. There has been a clear evolutionary process evident as the relationship between my father and me, from infancy to present, has constantly changed. Its development has been a major part of who I am today, and by reviewing our past, it helps to see where we are going.

When I Was an Infant . . .

Honestly, I don't remember much about when I was an infant. All I know about our relationship when I was at that age comes from pictures my mother keeps in a box down in her basement and the stories shared by my parents.

Sometimes I like to go down to the basement and go through that box, looking at mementos from that time I know existed but cannot remember. The white, dusty box contains items from when I was first introduced to this earth—including a rattler, spoon, and, of course, several baby pictures. The love shown in these pictures is so obvious that it still brings a smile to my face by just thinking about them.

I enjoy one picture in particular that was taken by my mom. It shows my dad and me lying on the bed together, taking a nap. My tiny head is touching my father's comparatively huge noggin as we face in towards each other. Our eyes are closed, and we are both sound asleep. There is a great amount of peace, innocence, and delicacy found in this photo, and it clearly shows the tenderness that my father showered on me, his new son.

During this stage of my life, my dad's role was caretaker, and I had no choice but to accept his love and concern. I was a fragile baby, and he treated me as just that. I trusted him in every way because I knew that he would cause me no harm. He could toss me up in the air with nothing but his hands to prevent me from hitting the floor, and I would just laugh and enjoy the ride. The amount of trust that an infant gives his or her parents is truly amazing, and I was no exception. Dad was my caretaker, and I knew would never do me any wrong.

WHEN I WAS A TODDLER . . .

Though many of the memories still remain fuzzy, I can remember and hold on to tightly to a few precious moments of my dad and me when I was a toddler. I remember when my dad would put me on his lap and bounce me up and down to the tune of "Mr. Dog," a song he had made up for Sam and me. It went like this:

> *Bom, bom, bom Mr. Dog*
> *Bom, bom, bom Mr. Dog*
> *Funny little nose*
> *Big brown hat*
> *The dog with the corncob pipe*
> *Whoo!*

Lyrically, the song was terrible, but for whatever reason, it brought a smile to my face whenever Dad would break into a round. I also recall playing Superman with him. My father would lie on his back and hold me up as high as he could with his arms and his legs so I could pretend that I was flying. He referred to it earlier as "wayuphigh."

This was also the period of my life when he first introduced sports to me. He would toss me a ball and I would try to catch it, usually failing. I would then attempt to throw it back to him, most of the time tossing it in the direction opposite what I intended.

As a toddler, my dad became my source of encouragement. He believed in me, and he still does to this day. He was half of the team (my mom being the other half) that motivated me to walk, talk, and throw the baseball. He was there cheering me on through all of my falls and spills and would never even think about berating me.

As I mentioned in previous chapters, this encouragement has continued even today. Just as when I was learning to walk, he is there motivating me during my errors, failures, and successes. This has always been vitally important to me: to have someone in my corner who I know will be behind me all the way. Fortunately for me, this is my father, and I attribute many of my successes to him and his belief in his son.

WHEN I WAS IN MY PRIMARY YEARS . . .

When I was in my primary years, my dad became my teacher. Sure, he helped with my homework, but he taught more important lessons than reading, writing, and how to multiply. During this time in my life, my father began to instill in me biblical values of right and wrong. Though many of the morals I learned were the basic commandments concerning stealing, lying, and killing, a solid foundation for a deeper, more powerful relationship with God was being established. He taught of God's love for me and the world that He created. We sat down and read Bible stories together so that I might start engraving Scripture in my heart and mind.

Though my father was a pastor, he did not solely rely on the church to teach me God's love, values, and Scriptures. As I believe every parent should, he took it upon himself to teach me these things.

I think most readers can relate when I say that during this point in time, I viewed my dad as the most incredible man in the world, and I listened to whatever he had to say. He was my hero, and I would believe whatever he told me. So when he read of David and Goliath, I was there on the edge of my seat, waiting to see if David was going to defeat the giant. When he told me that God loved me and wanted to have a relationship with me, my ears and eyes were wide open. A Sunday school teacher could have taught me these things, but it would never have had the impact of having my dad tell me. Because Dad decided to take on the role of teacher, my young mind was filled with thoughts of God and His Word.

When I Was a Teenager . . .

When I was a teenager, the only role I thought my dad took on was disciplinarian, and I gave him plenty of opportunities to exert his power over me. However, now I realize that the most important role he played during this stage of my life was a model of how to live out the Christian life. I feel that during my teenage years I began to understand that not everyone has a dad like mine; something was different. I noticed that other dads did not act and treat the family the same as my father did. Before this point, I guess I never really took notice, but when I did, I started to pay more attention. I studied how he handled himself in every situation, from family to work to church. He was becoming my role model for how I would live life in the future. Much of this book comes from memories made during this time in my life. The teenage years are crucial to how a child develops into adulthood. Many of the habits and choices made during this stage will follow for the remainder of one's life.

And though it may seem difficult to maintain a decent relationship between father and son or daughter due primarily to the "weirdness" of the teenager, parents must never give up; they must never stop pursuing.

While I do not classify myself as the most difficult teenager, I did have times when I am sure my father would have liked to disown me. Luckily, he never did. He decided to chase after a close relationship with me no matter how much I attempted to distance myself. As I watched him do this, I eventually drew closer to him as well. Once again, I was watching him; waiting to see what he would do. My teenage images of him will remain with me for the rest of my life, and I will use it as a guide to live my life in such a way that will please our heavenly Father.

When I Was in College . . .

When I was in college, my father began to evolve into something new, something different in my eyes. I suddenly began not only to see him as a parent but also as a human being (and it only took eighteen years). I guess that this is not uncommon. For some reason the college years make us realize that our parents are not a couple of crazies out to deny us any fun in life. We begin to understand the reason for the curfews and dating limitations, and we actually begin to adapt these ideals into our own, now "free," lives. We start to understand that we were not as wise as we once thought we were in high school.

College was a time when I began to really open up to my father. I seemed to care more what he thought and started wanting a deeper relationship than I had before, probably what he had wanted all along. Our few phone calls throughout the week kept us in touch with what was going on in both of our worlds. Talking to my dad stopped becoming such a hassle and became an event I enjoyed. I began to seek his wisdom in different areas, and took more to heart any advice that he would give. Yes, suddenly he became a human, one that I admired and respected.

NOW THAT I AM A YOUNG ADULT . . .

Now that I am a young adult and away from my parents' immediate care, the evolution that began in college has continued to develop even more fully. While our relationship and my view of my father have not changed significantly since my college days, my dad has now become my closest friend and primary mentor.

It's funny, now I call him more than he ever called me while I was in college. Whenever I need someone's advice, he is the one I turn to. I ask him a wide array of questions to pick his mind, to gather his advice. Out of nowhere he has become the great and wise guru in all aspects of life. I heed his instruction now more than ever in my life, and I treasure his words like gold. The life that he has led as a husband and father has become the life that I admire and desire to imitate. Those are pretty big words, and I can only hope that my future children will say the same about me.

Even more than a mentor, I enjoy my dad as a friend. He has been able to put aside the parenting role and replace it with something greater, more meaningful. Friends are tremendous influences in all of our lives, and by his taking on the role of my friend, he is able to influence me more than anyone else.

"Hey, Dad, when I am in town, do you want to go out to get something to eat, just hangout?"

"Sure, Art. I would love to."

This has become a regular request of mine whenever I come to visit my parents. There is something about sitting down with my father and having a good conversation that is satisfying and peaceful. I enjoy it more than he will ever realize. There is a connection there that cannot be given to me by anyone else. I tell him about what is going on in my life, and he tells me about his. That is all that it takes; it is simple, yet nothing can compare.

As our relationship continues to evolve, I get excited about where it will take us and how deep it can go. The places we have been and the times we have had are moments that I would never take back. Soon, there will be grandchildren, and Thom Rainer will not only be a father and husband but also a grandfather. I look forward to how our relationship will evolve even further. I don't know exactly how everything will turn out between my father and me, but I do know that the first twenty-five years have laid an incredible foundation for what lies ahead. As we both enter into new eras of our lives, I hope for the best, and pray that God will continue to bless us both in our relationship with one another, just as He has already done.

FINAL THOUGHTS

Now that the book is coming to a close, I look back on what I have written and realize that the words I have put on these pages do not even come close to describing how I feel about my dad. My description of the admiration, appreciation, and love that I have for my father has come up woefully short. This tribute to a great man in my life is somehow going to have to be left incomplete. Sadly, I don't know what else to do, and I don't know what else to write. I think I have come to conclude through this whole process that there are some things that you just can't express with words alone, and what my father means to me is one of those inexpressible realities.

Yet at the same time I realize that this is the beauty of the relationship; there is something there that neither of us can express fully in words, but we understand it just the same. It is a unique bond built over time, and I know it will become even stronger.

I have been blessed to raise Dad.

And may I be the type of father who will bless his children as well.

And when the final chapters are written in my life, may my children say with joy, "Raising Dad was one of our greatest blessings."

— A Father's Perspective —

Would I change anything about being a dad? In the larger scale of things, the answer is no. I have been blessed beyond measure, and I would not dare tamper with the gifts I have been given.

Yet, from another perspective, there is much that I would change. Indeed, one of the primary reasons I wrote this book with Art is to share lessons of fatherhood: the good, the bad, and the ugly.

Art took a journey to the recent past to review the raising of Dad from his perspective. I will do the same.

The Precious Gift of Life

My memories of the births of my three boys are vivid. I was there in the delivery room, a fairly new development at that time. With each of my sons, I remember the nurse giving me my son to hold. It was an experience for the ages.

I looked into those newly opened eyes. I held their tiny hands. I kissed my sons gently on the forehead. And I had the biggest lump in my throat.

This is my son. In my arms is a life that my wife and I have made. This child will grow in my home. He will change my life. This is my son.

I had a myriad of emotions. And when we brought Art home for his two-year-old brother to meet, we put the new baby carefully in the arms of his big brother. Sam was nervous at first, and then he began to calm down. He too looked into the eyes of his little brother. "I like him," Sam said.

We were glad he did!

I have never taken for granted the incredible gifts of life God has given me in my three sons. When they were infants, I would look at them for long periods of time in total awe. *This is my son. This is a child that Nellie Jo and I have given life. This is my son.*

But I did have my struggles.

No one ever gave me a book or taught me a course on how to enjoy babies at three in the morning. "Thom," my wife would mumble, "it's your turn to get the baby." My turn? I had to work the next day. I needed my sleep. My turn?

Likewise, changing diapers was a "lovely" experience. We could not afford disposable diapers, so I learned to use pins on cloth diapers. That part was OK. But taking the soiled diapers and cleaning them in the toilet was another matter altogether.

It is easy to look back on the days when the boys were babies and have moments of longing and nostalgia. But having babies in the house was tough, especially for my wife, who shouldered 90 percent of the load.

Honesty compels me to recall numerous moments of weariness and irritability. I remember pleading with our babies on more than one occasion: "Please go to sleep," only to get a smile from a wide awake child.

I really wish I could say that I was a perfect, patient, and long-suffering father. But I was not. I often snapped at my wife. I often resented the babies' terrible schedules. I was far from perfect.

If I had the opportunity to do it over again, I hope that I would have a better perspective. I hope that I would understand how incredibly brief is the time of having a baby in the house. I hope I would appreciate the gift of life even more.

I know I will do better with my grandchildren. Their fathers will have them deposited immediately into their arms at the first hint of difficulty. Ah, the joy of loving babies with none of the responsibilities!

TODDLERS AND FATHERHOOD

A toddler is a baby who has discovered mobility and original sin.

OK, I'm exaggerating again. But there is a hint of truth. A baby can't go anywhere, but a toddler loves to experience and discover the world with newfound mobility.

I really began to see my boys' personalities develop at this age. Sam was focused and intense. Jess was compassionate and easy-going. Art was . . . gone. We discovered quickly that our middle son was an independent spirit seeking to discover new lands to conquer. He compelled my wife to invest in child leashes—then when Art was in the mall, he could go no further than the full extension of the leash.

I loved this stage of development. I started getting a bit playful with the boys. I would toss them in the air, much to their delight and to their mother's horror. I would wrestle them on the floor and tickle them silly. I would wait for Art to give me his half-smile and insist, "Do it again, Daddy." I would delight when little Sam tried to hold me down. And I loved it when Jess started laughing even before I began tickling him.

I love those boys.

But I was a busy dad. Too busy.

If I could do it over, I would see that those vitally important tasks weren't nearly as important as I thought. I would have realized that my boys were toddlers for such a brief season. My wife knew that. She did well. But I didn't. I was just too busy.

And that busyness carried into their childhood.

THE CHILDHOOD YEARS:
CONFESSIONS OF A BUSY FATHER

I love St. Petersburg, Florida. I was the pastor of the Azalea Baptist Church there in the late 1980s. I loved that church too. I look back on those days as some of the best of my life. The boys were in childhood, heavily involved in school, church, and sports. And we were living in paradise.

Though my wife was the chief chauffeur for the boys, I occasionally took on that task. I loved the drive from our house to the boys' school. You had a picture-perfect view of the emerald waters of the Gulf of Mexico and the sugar-white sands of the beach. On occasion, I would tell the boys to bring their swimsuits in the car with them because I wanted to take them to the beach after school.

I still remember the light in their faces and the big wide smiles. They had something to look forward to all day. Dad was taking them to the beach.

I remember the excitement when I picked them up from school. And I remember those late afternoon hours on Madeira Beach. We had a blast.

Now here's the sad part of the story. I can remember most of those afternoons because I did it so infrequently. I was busy. I led a growing congregation. The demands were heavy. The expectations were high. And too often I let other people become more important than my own sons.

Let me illustrate my mixed-up priorities in my boys' childhood. All three of my sons spoke at my inauguration as president of LifeWay Christian Resources in 2006. Jess spoke first. He told about a trip he made with me when I was a pastor in St. Petersburg. He recalled how just the two of us made the four-hundred-mile trip to Eufaula, Alabama, where I was to preach at a revival.

Jess spoke with such joy. The trip and our one-on-one time were obviously special, as he was able to recall details seventeen years later. I, too, was caught up in his recollection of the father-son adventure.

But when I began doing my outline for this book, I had an entirely different emotion. This time I began to question why trips and times like that were more rare than common. How many opportunities like that did I blow because I was just too busy? I really don't want to know the answer to that question. Sometimes denial is the least painful path.

I do have great memories of the boys' childhood. But I know there could have been many more.

The Not-So-Terrible Teens

None of the three boys were perfect teenagers. Believe me, Nellie Jo and I did have our moments of exasperation. But on the whole, I consider their teen years a blessing.

My wife and I did have to accept the perspective of our teenage boys that their parents' IQ had been cut in half. We did realize that we were not the brightest creatures in the world to them.

But the teen years were rich. We began developing a new type of relationship with our sons. They were not yet adults, but they were more adults than children. The Rainer home became the hangout for teens on our side of town. The boys who came into our home are still some of our dearest friends today.

I am not certain how our place became a destination spot for teenage boys, but I am glad it did. Not only did I come to love those boys, I actually got to spend more time with my own sons because they were home more. Yes, our house showed the wear of a decade of teens. And yes, our budget was strained as we tried to feed the insatiable appetites of growing boys.

But we wouldn't change a thing. I have to say with all modesty that the Rainer home for teens was one of my success stories.

But let me share one aspect of the boys' teen years that I just didn't get: girls.

I could tell how a relationship was going according to a son's disposition.

"Good morning, son."

"Unhhhnn."

"How did your night go last night?"

"OK."

"Is something wrong?"

"Why do you always ask me if something is wrong? Can't you just leave me alone?"

Nellie Jo and I would look at each other knowingly. Girlfriend problems.

And I wish I could tell you that I was a font of wisdom. I never have figured out girls.

So my wife and I did the only thing we knew to do. We prayed. We prayed that same prayer that we have said since our boys were babies: "Lord, please give them godly Christian wives." And those prayers have been answered with the great blessings of Sarah, Erin, and Rachel. But as I promised, I will talk more about them in the last chapter.

THOSE COLLEGE YEARS

While Art confessed to some times of rebellious behavior in college, I really have no major complaint about the boys during this phase of their lives. To the contrary, my relationship deepened with each son. They were becoming men, and I relished every conversation I had with them. I cherished every moment I spent with them. And though I never told them,

I often canceled out-of-town engagements if I knew they were going to be home.

And I never considered such rearrangements of my schedule an imposition or sacrifice. To the contrary, I enjoy my boys so much that there is nothing I would rather do than spend time with them.

It was during those college years that the boys began responding to "I love you, son" with "I love you, Dad." Indeed they even began initiating expressions of love.

I could tell that my sons were becoming men. There was some sadness to see the childhood and teen years disappear, but I knew that only better days were ahead.

Adult Sons and an Aging Dad

I am more than a half-century old. When I was born in 1955, the Beatles had not even become a group. Few Americans knew of a nation called Vietnam. The Watergate Hotel would not be built for another twelve years. And John F. Kennedy was the new and young senator from Massachusetts.

Time has passed so quickly.

I treasure these days with my sons more than ever. I listen to them and heed their advice as much as they do my own. I share my dreams and visions and listen to theirs. They are my sons, but they are also my best friends.

I try to be careful not to intrude on their new families. We are no longer the only parents in their lives, and Nellie Jo and I respect the time our boys spend with their wives' families.

The good old days? I am living them right now.

I am the most blessed man on earth with the greatest sons in the world.

I have three daughters-in-law who are precious gifts to me. And Nellie Jo finally has girls to even things up.

You can't get me to stop talking about my boys. I have messed up as a father on many occasions, but God's grace and their forgiveness have been abundant. If I had my life to live over again, I would make some changes because I failed much. But I wouldn't change the big picture. I would still ask for three sons named Art, Jess, and Sam. I would still marry my girlfriend, Nellie Jo. And I would still choose the same friends I have today.

Art has taken me on this journey, and it has brought back a flood of memories. Art has raised Dad well. I am so blessed.

And the lessons I have learned have been many. Will you join me in this final chapter as I share with you my lessons from fatherhood?

~~~~~~

The Legacy of a Dad: Twelve Lessons of Fatherhood

by Thom S. Rainer

Art has raised his Dad well. I recently did an interview for an online publication. One of the questions was: "Who has been the greatest leadership influence in your life?" Without hesitation, I wrote: "My three sons: Sam, Art, and Jess."

Fatherhood has been an educational journey that no school could provide. I have learned so much. And even to this day, I listen to my sons. They may think that I am offering them words of wisdom, but I am learning from them as well.

I think you have read clearly that I do not see myself as the great expert on fatherhood. I hope I have been transparent and honest in my self-assessment, especially with the weaknesses and faults that I have.

On the one hand, this book has been one of my greatest joys. On the other hand, it has been painful. I have been reminded again and again how I could have done better, how I should have done better.

Nevertheless, I accept the grace that came with Art's rose-colored perspectives. I spoke with a friend and fellow father recently, telling him about the grace that Art demonstrated in this book. He responded, "Yeah, it is amazing that our kids love us anyway." That's how I feel. Art, Jess, and Sam love me anyway.

I also realize that the far superior parent in our family is my wife, Nellie Jo. I have never seen such sacrificial and unconditional love flow from one human to another. She is the true instrument of God who raised our three sons so well.

But this is a book about fatherhood. At the end of the day, I have several lessons that I have learned about the great challenge of being a dad. Thank you for allowing this fellow struggler the opportunity to share these lessons.

Lesson 1: Children Are Precious Gifts from God

If we parents ever fully recognize the incredible gift we have been given in our children, our attitude about them will be one of unceasing praise. I realize that not every couple has been given children. And I realize that I do not deserve my sons any more than husbands and wives who have not been blessed with children. They are gifts of grace. Undeserved and unmerited.

Have you ever assessed a situation and realized how completely blessed you are? That is how I feel about my boys. One of the reasons that I have not failed completely as a father is that my sons know how much I treasure them. They have a confidence and assurance that they are wanted. They know that I see them as precious gifts from God. They know that I feel like I am the most blessed man in the world to have them as my sons.

On those occasions where I have been weary and irritable, I often remind myself of this gift. Such thinking really puts minor issues in perspective. Children are gifts. Never, ever forget that truth.

LESSON 2: WE MUST LOVE OUR CHILDREN UNCONDITIONALLY, AND THEY MUST KNOW IT

You have heard the story of Art's "confessions" in San Diego in this book. It was an important moment for my son. It was a turning point in his life spiritually and in his relationship with me. He felt a great relief by clearing the air.

That moment was important for me as well. It gave me the opportunity to emphasize again that my love for Art was unconditional. There is absolutely nothing he could do to make me stop loving him. He could hurt me. He could disappoint me. He could even reject me. But my love would not go away.

A child who grows up with unconditional love is more secure and more joyous. He or she does not have to earn the love of a parent. It is there no matter what.

The analogy of the heavenly Father's love for us through Christ is a fit comparison. We did not earn His love. We did not merit His love. But we can be secure in His love. The apostle Paul said it clearly in Ephesians 2:8–9: "For by grace you are saved through faith, and this is not from yourselves; it is God's gift—not from works, so that no one can boast." Paul spoke of the security of Christ's love in Romans 8:38–39: "For I am persuaded that neither death nor life, nor angels nor rulers, nor things present, nor things to come, nor powers, nor height, nor depth, nor any other created thing will have the power to separate us from the love of God that is in Christ Jesus our Lord!"

Our children can take a lot from this world if they know that Mom and Dad are there for them no matter what. The love of Christ is the greatest security. And the unconditional love of a parent is a child's greatest earthly security.

LESSON 3: LOVE YOUR CHILDREN'S MOTHER

The ten-year-old boy sat in my office. I was a pastor in Kentucky. After a few minutes of casual conversation, I finally got him to tell me why he wanted to see me. "Dan" put his hands to his face and started crying profusely: "My daddy doesn't love my mama anymore."

I was heartbroken with the heartbroken boy. I swept Dan into my arms and let him cry it out. I hurt so much for the little fellow. Dan's parents divorced a few months later.

I am not a perfect father. Not close. And I am not a perfect husband. Far from it. But do you know what Art, Sam, and Jess know? Despite my imperfections as a husband, despite my stupid anger, despite my self-centeredness, I love their mother. I am with her until death do us part. My sons can live in the assurance and the confidence that, not only do I love them, I love and adore my wife, their mother.

Nellie Jo and I are blessed with three daughters. God gave Art a wife named Sarah, Sam a wife named Erin, and Jess a wife named Rachel. These three young ladies are the answers to our prayers. They are beautiful physically but, more importantly, they are beautiful spiritually. And they love our sons. And we love them for that. I pray that my boys will show their children what it is like to love and adore their mothers.

Art said that his knowledge of the certainty of my love for Nellie Jo made a big difference in his life. Last weekend Nellie Jo and I had lunch with Art and his wife, Sarah. At the conclusion of the meal, I saw Art put his arm around Sarah. It was like I was looking in a mirror (a much younger and lighter image of course). He put his arm around his wife just the way I do with my wife. I pray that the love I have had for his mother will be a factor in his own marriage being blessed and joyous.

LESSON 4: TIME CAN NEVER BE RECAPTURED

Art told the story earlier of his baseball team when he was seven years old. One day I was coaching at third base when Art hit the ball into the infield. Seeing that he was a certain out at first base, he did not run all the way to the base, a cardinal sin in baseball. The coach gave him several sentences of reprimand, which irked me. I was about to say something to the coach when Art came running across the field, holding back tears. He looked at me with hurt all over his face and said, "Daddy, that coach hurt my feelings."

I swept my son into my arms. He already knew that he had made a baseball mistake, so I did not dwell on that issue. After a few minutes, Art was fine, having fun again with his teammates.

Why did I tell that story? I simply remember how good I felt when I held my son. And I remember how great it was to be able to soothe hurt feelings with a hug and a few sentences. I also remember how much fun I had coaching the team with both Sam and Art on it.

That was yesterday . . . or so it seems. Actually it was nearly twenty years ago. Where has the time gone?

The time that we have our children at home is so incredibly brief. Make the most of it. Enjoy each year of their lives. Celebrate each moment.

It will be over before you know it.

LESSON 5: DISCIPLINE IS A SIGN OF LOVE

One of the persons on the dedication page is Peggy Dutton. She loved our boys almost as if they were her own grandchildren. Peggy was my assistant when I was a pastor in St. Petersburg, and she quickly became a member of our family.

Peggy graciously looked after our boys so that Nellie Jo and I could have an occasional night out. She knew how to take care of three rambunctious boys. If they ever got out of line, she would shout, "I'm going to jerk a knot in you."

Now Peggy never did jerk that knot. I don't think she knew how. But my boys knew that "Miss Peggy" meant business, and she had full permission to discipline them.

Neither Nellie Jo nor I enjoyed disciplining our sons, but we did so anyway. To do less was to tell our boys that we didn't care what they did, that we had no boundaries. They did not like the discipline when they were children, but now they tell us how much they appreciate it.

The writer of Hebrews tells us that discipline is a sign of love, and he points to God's love as a disciplining love in Hebrews 12:5–11:

> My son, do not take the Lord's discipline
> lightly, or faint when you are reproved by Him;
> for the Lord disciplines the one He loves, and
> punishes every son whom He receives. Endure
> it as discipline: God is dealing with you as sons.
> For what son is there whom a father does not
> discipline? But if you are without discipline—
> which all receive—then you are illegitimate
> children and not sons. Furthermore, we had
> natural fathers discipline us, and we respected
> them. Shouldn't we submit even more to the
> Father of spirits and live? For they disciplined
> us for a short time based on what seemed good
> to them, but He does it for our benefit, so
> that we can share His holiness. No discipline
> seems enjoyable at the time, but painful. Later
> on, however, it yields the fruit of peace and
> righteousness to those who have been trained by it.

There were times when I was tempted to avoid the hassle and pain of disciplining Art, Jess, and Sam. I am glad that I avoided that temptation.

LESSON 6: ENCOURAGEMENT BUILDS UP A CHILD

Oldest Sam was driving his truck, and I was in the passenger seat. "Dad, what one piece of advice would you give me on being a father?" Now that question really hit me for a couple reasons. First, my son was really asking for my advice. I love this adult-son age where they really listen to me. Second, Sam is not yet a father. But he is anticipating the day when he and Erin will be blessed with children.

I can't say that I thought through the answer with any great depth, but the answer that came most quickly to my mind was: "Encourage your kids. Let them know how proud you are of them. Many children go through their entire lives seeking and not getting their parents' approval."

Sam responded, "Yeah, Dad, that's what you have done with Art, Jess, and me. And it has worked!"

The blessing. That's what a parent's approval is. And for whatever reasons, fathers seem to withhold such encouragement and approval more than mothers do. I thank God that I learned the lesson of the blessing.

LESSON 7: COMMUNICATE THE BLESSING WITH WORDS AND TOUCH

Perhaps this lesson could be included in the lesson above. I simply want to emphasize that even if our children know we love them and that we are proud of them, they need to hear it. They need to feel with our hugs. When they are young, the physical interaction with children is critical. When they are older, we must still keep hugging them.

Art made this point crystal clear in this book. He remembers the words I *said*. He remembers the embrace of his father. We parents cannot assume that our children know we love them; we must tell them and show them.

Lesson 8: Talk to Your Children

I love it. I absolutely love it. My sons still want to talk to me. Yesterday Art called to talk to me about this book. Sam called to talk to me about work. Jess called two days earlier just to catch up.

My boys can call my cell phone at almost any time. They know that I am the president of this big company, but they know they can get in touch with me quickly. Most of the time I will answer their calls on the spot. Otherwise, I get back to them quickly. I am honored beyond measure that those boys still want to talk to me.

I think I instilled this desire early in their lives. I let them know that there was no such thing as a stupid question and that there were no subjects that were out of bounds. We *really* had some interesting discussions. Some of them were theological. Some of them were blunt talks about the "facts of life." Others were about sports, girls, politics, morals, clothes, careers, hobbies, places to live, places to go, and the list goes on.

At the risk of redundancy, I will remind you that I was far from perfect. But I think the reason that my boys desire to talk to me today is because our conversations began when they were very young.

Lesson 9: Fun and Humor Is Healthy

The Rainer house was a fun place to be. I think that's why we became a hangout on the east side of town. All three of my boys have a great sense of humor.

Our three sons like to joke with one another. They especially enjoy making fun of their old man. Because they had

to endure hundreds of my sermons and speeches, they frequently would imitate my mannerisms and frequently repeated
phrases. Their mother enjoyed popping paper bags behind them
when they were not aware she was in the room.

The Rainer home was just fun, and I have to believe that
such an environment contributed to the emotional health of
the three boys.

Art is the best in the family with one-liners. He does not
have to premeditate on them; they just come naturally. And
the wives they have brought into the Rainer family have joined
right in with the laughter and humor.

Lesson 10: Admit Your Mistakes

Art and his brothers have taught me much as they have
raised their dad. My natural and sinful tendency was to speak
quickly and harshly when one of the boys was out of line. On
one occasion, when Jess was seven years old, he said something
to me that I felt was wrong. I quickly responded in anger and
sent him to his room. But the look of hurt on his face as he left
to go to his room told me that I had reacted too quickly and
too much out of anger.

After a few minutes, I realized that Jess's comments to
me were really not that bad. Indeed, my weary state at the
time probably made a big deal out of an innocent comment.
I marched myself up to Jess's room, where he was still hurting. I told him that I was wrong, that I had responded out
of anger, and that he really had done nothing to warrant my
response.

Jess was still a bit hurt, and he wasn't sure how to respond
to me. I looked him in the eye, put my hand on his shoulders,

and said, "Look buddy, Dad was wrong. Will you forgive me?" He nodded his assent, and I gave him the biggest hug and offered to take him for a treat.

I blew it many times as a father. But my boys have taught me to think before I speak and to be willing to ask for forgiveness when I was wrong. They have indeed raised Dad well.

LESSON 11: KNOW WHEN TO LET GO, KNOW WHEN TO HOLD

Do you remember the chapter on transparency? Art rightly recognized me as a transparent father. Indeed, there were not many things that I did not share with my sons. And there were not many emotions I left unchecked.

On the one hand, this transparency is good. My boys knew where I stood on almost all issues. They knew they could get clear and non-evasive answers from me. And they knew how I felt at almost all times. There was no doubt how Dad was feeling in the Rainer home.

On the other hand, I was often transparent to a fault. Kids need to be kids, and they do not need to be exposed to every feeling and concern parents have. I needed to protect them from the harsh world more than I did, instead of letting them hear almost every fear and problem with which I struggled.

Some parents never let their children see the real mom and dad. And some parents let their kids see too much. I was guilty of the latter.

LESSON 12: THERE IS NOTHING MORE IMPORTANT THAN A CHILD'S ETERNITY

"Lord, please look over our sons. Keep them in Your protective and loving hands. Help us to be the type of parents that show Your love. And we pray for the salvation of our sons. We ask that they hear clearly one day the gospel message, and that they accept and follow Your Son Jesus."

Those words, or words similar to those, were prayed by Nellie Jo and me on a regular basis. We do want the best for our sons in this life. But this life is so incredibly brief. Our most fervent prayer was for each of the boys to become a Christian so that their eternities would be secure.

God has answered our prayers. Very few dads have had the incredible privilege to do what I did. I baptized each of my sons after they became followers of Christ. Those were moments that I cherished, moments that moved me to tears.

One of the most moving stories in Scripture is the story of the death of King David's baby boy in 2 Samuel 12:21–23: "His servants asked him, 'What did you just do? While the baby was alive, you fasted and wept, but when he died, you got up and ate food.' He answered, 'While the baby was alive, I fasted and wept because I thought, "Who knows? The LORD may be gracious to me and let him live." But now that he is dead, why should I fast? Can I bring him back again? I'll go to him, but he will never return to me.'"

David said with total assurance that even though his son could not return to him, he would one day go to his son. And I know that one day, at that great and final reunion, I will be with my sons for eternity. That is the hope that we have all found in Jesus Christ.

Though I was imperfect, I tried to model Christ to my sons. I wanted them to see Him in both my words and actions. I wanted them to have the freedom to talk with me about anything, especially spiritual matters.

God answered our prayers. The most important gift a child can receive is the gift of salvation in Christ. And I thank God that He used Nellie Jo and me as His instruments in their eternities.

"It Is Time"

I really don't want this book to end. It has been one of the greatest joys of my life, even though it has been a painful reminder of my many failures.

In 1985, when all three boys were still preschool age, I came across a prayer written by General Douglas MacArthur for his son. Ironically, his son's name was Arthur. I liked much of what the prayer offered, but there was something that made me uncomfortable. In the prayer, General MacArthur frequently used the phrase, "Make me a son . . ." and then he would describe to God what attributes he wanted in his son.

Why was I uncomfortable with the prayer? It finally dawned on me. My prayer was not for the kind of son God would make for me, but the kind of father He would make of me. If I were the type of father that pleased God, then my sons might follow my example. So I rewrote the prayer on my electric typewriter and cut the paper to fit a frame. I have kept that frame and prayer on my desk in every place I have been from 1985 to this day. May I share that prayer with you?

A Prayer
by Thom S. Rainer

FROM AN IMPERFECT FATHER
FOR HIS THREE PRICELESS SONS

Make me the father, O Lord, who will show my sons the strength to face weakness, the courage to face fear, the grace to accept honest defeat, and the humility and gentleness to accept victory.

Make me the father who will show my sons not a path of ease and comfort, but the ability to accept the challenge of stress and difficulty. Use me, I pray, to be the example of one who can stand up in the storm, and there learn compassion for those who fail.

Make me the father who will teach his sons the value of a clear heart and a high goal; to master themselves before they seek to master other men; to learn to laugh, yet never forget how to cry; to reach into the future without forgetting the past.

Make me the father, O Lord, who will show my sons enough of a sense of humor so that they will always be serious, but never take themselves too seriously. Give them humility so that they will always remember the simplicity of true greatness, the open mind of true wisdom, the meekness of true strength.

And after all these things are theirs, add for
me, I pray, the wisdom to show them the
dubious value of titles, positions, money, and
material gain; and the eternal value of prayer,
the Holy Bible, a Christian home, and a saving
relationship with your Son Jesus Christ.

Then I, their father, will dare to whisper,
"I have not lived in vain."

You see, Art, Sam, and Jess are three of the most precious
gifts I have ever been given. I love those boys so much, and
I never, ever want to take those gifts for granted.

You have honored Art and me by allowing us to take you on
a very personal journey. It has been our prayer that our stories,
trials, and victories would speak to you to help you be a better
father, a better mother, or just a better person.

Life is so incredibly brief. We are stewards of the time and
the gifts we have been given. Soon, very soon, life will be done.
We can only pray that we leave behind a legacy that makes a
difference.

I mentioned earlier in this book about the great privilege
I had to be at my father's bedside when he died. My family and
I made weekend round trips of 1,200 miles from Louisville,
Kentucky, to Union Springs, Alabama, to be with my father as
his conditioned worsened.

As I was packing for one of those long weekend trips, I got
a call from my mother. "Thom, you probably should pack for a
few extra days and bring clothes for the funeral. It doesn't look
like your dad will make it through the weekend. It is time."

It is time.

At the young age of sixty-two, it was his time.

So brief. So very brief was his time.

He did die shortly after we arrived. And I said good-bye to a godly father whom I knew I would see again.

Though I cannot presume upon God's providence, I really hope to precede my sons and wife in death. And though I do not know how my life will end, it is possible that Nellie Jo may make a phone call to Art, Jess, and Sam and say, "It is time."

I hope I will make the transition with Christlike strength. I pray that I can be an example for my sons one last time. And I pray that the legacy I leave them will be passed on to their sons and daughters and beyond.

Life is so brief.

Art and his brothers have raised their dad well.

May those who come behind us find us faithful.

Soon and very soon, it will be time.

Appendix

~~~~~~~

Questions for Discussion

Chapter 1: Raising Dad: Memories and More

1. How can a parent become intentional in memory making?
2. Why are some parents too busy for their children?
3. How should parents evaluate a potential relocation to another town? Should they include their children in the discussion?
4. How can parents avoid the tension of giving time to their work and giving time to their children?

Chapter 2: When a Father Is Like the Father

1. How can parents create intentional prayer time with their children?
2. In what ways do Christian parents sometimes fail to let their "walk" match their "talk"?

3. How can we help our children to share their faith?
4. What are some creative ways to study the Bible with our children?

Chapter 3: When a Man Loves a Woman

1. How do parents show children that they love their spouse?
2. What do your children hear when their parents talk to each other?
3. How can a spouse show love to another spouse in difficult times? How does this commitment affect their children?
4. How does respect or lack of respect for your spouse affect your children?

Chapter 4: Three Gifts: Support, Encouragement, and Love

1. How can parents demonstrate healthy pride in their children?
2. Name several ways we offer encouragement to our children.
3. How can a lack of support and encouragement from a parent to a child affect that child in his or her adult years?
4. How can we encourage our children when they have experienced disappointment or failure?

Chapter 5: The Lost Art of Discipline

1. How can a parent determine the right type of discipline for a child?
2. Do you think types of discipline should be different for different children?

3. How does the concept of "tough love" apply to disciplining children?

4. What would you do, as a parent, if you felt that you had been too harsh on a child when you disciplined him or her?

Chapter 6: The Family of Fun

1. What do you think God's perspective of fun is?

2. What might preclude a parent from having fun with his or her child?

3. How can we be intentional about having fun in our families?

4. Name the most fun you ever had in your family. Why was that such a great moment? How can such moments be repeated?

Chapter 7: Love: Saying It and Showing It

1. What are the similarities and differences between the ways you demonstrate love to your children and how your parents demonstrated love to you?

2. How can parents clearly communicate unconditional love to their children?

3. Why is a hug so important to a child?

4. How should parents respond if their teenage children resist hugs and are embarrassed when they are told verbally "I love you"?

Chapter 8: That Time Thing

1. What are the reasons that some parents fail to give their children adequate time? What can be done to overcome these problems?

2. Why is it important to our children for husbands and wives to spend time together?

3. Name some creative ways to spend time with your children.

4. How should a parent respond if a teenage child expresses that he or she does not want to spend time with the parent?

Chapter 9: The Transparent Father

1. When is it appropriate for a parent to be transparent? When is it not?

2. Do you feel that you are a spiritual role model for your children? Do they see Christ clearly in you? Why? Why not?

3. Should our children see us cry? Why or why not?

4. How can a parent's transparency help his or her child to be more secure?

Chapter 10: A Time to Let Go

1. How are some parents too strict with their children?

2. How are some parents too lenient with their children?

3. Do many parents today fail to teach their children the value of a good work ethic? Why or why not?

4. Why are many children unprepared for adulthood today?

Chapter 11: Evolution of a Dad

1. What are a child's greatest needs as a toddler?

2. What are a child's greatest needs as preteen?

3. What are a child's greatest needs as a teenager?

4. What are a child's greatest needs as an adult?